USDA United States Department of Agriculture

Climate Change Edition 2014

I0411837

Natural IQ

Investigating Questions About Nature

Inside

U.S. Forest Service

Southern Research Station

General Technical Report - SRS-183

Natural IQ

Investigating Questions about Climate

Forest Service, U.S. Department of Agriculture, Asheville, NC 28804

Produced by the Southern Research Station of the Forest Service (U.S. Department of Agriculture) and the Cradle of Forestry in America Interpretive Association

Natural IQ Production Staff

Babs McDonald, Forest Service, U.S. Department of Agriculture
Jessica Nickelsen, Cradle of Forestry in America Interpretive Association
Julia Dobish, Cradle of Forestry in America Interpretive Association
Elissa Riley, Cradle of Forestry in America Interpretive Association
Michelle Andrews, University of Georgia
Emily Melear-Daniels, Cradle of Forestry in America Interpretive Association

Graphic Designer

Nickola Dudley, Blacksburg, VA
http://nickoladudley.zenfolio.com/

Illustrator

Stephanie Pfeiffer, Athens, GA

Cartographer

Lindsay Gnann, Athens, GA

Forest Service, U.S. Department of Agriculture

Tom Tidwell, Chief
Jimmy L. Reaves, Deputy Chief, Research and Development
Jim Hubbard, Deputy Chief, State and Private Forestry
William Lange, Acting Staff Director, Science Quality Services
Kristen Nelson, Acting Staff Director, Conservation Education
Rob Doudrick, Director, Southern Research Station
Jennifer Plyler, Assistant Director for Science Delivery, Southern Research Station
Kier Klepzig, Assistant Director, Southern Research Station
Steve McNulty, Climate Change Exhibit Advisor, Southern Research Station

Cradle of Forestry in America Interpretive Association

Carlton Murrey, Executive Director
Adam DeWitte, Director of Education
Jennifer Grantham, Chair

USDA Forest Service Scientists Highlighted in this Edition of *Natural IQ*

Scott Goodrick, Southern Research Station
Qinfeng Guo, Southern Research Station
Stephanie Laseter, Southern Research Station
Evan Mercer, Southern Research Station
Chelcy Ford Miniat, Southern Research Station
John Stanturf, Southern Research Station
James Vose, Southern Research Station

Collaborating Scientists

Janaki Alavalapati, Virginia Polytechnic Institute and State University
Arthur Chappelka, Auburn University
Dafeng Hui, Tennessee State University
Pankaj Lal, Montclair State University
Hong Qian, Illinois State Museum
Hanqin Tian, Auburn University

With thanks to

Project Learning Tree

Contents

Features

PHOTO BY TERRY SOHL.

Join Us in Being Green!

To reduce the amount of paper used to produce the *Natural IQ,* the following sections are now available exclusively on the *Natural Inquirer* Web site, http://www.naturalinquirer.org. These resources can be found with the Southern United States Climate Change edition and on the "Educational Resources" pages.

- Note to Educators

- Lesson Plan

- Reflection Section Answer Guide

- Individual Article Education Standards Correlations

Editorial Review Board

Ms. Lewis's 7th grade class, Rosman Middle School, Brevard, North Carolina

I think you should put different colors in the magazine other than blue and white. I also like how you put Web sites on the back of the magazine.

The most important thing I learned was that we can manage trees and how much water they are taking in from streams. I think it is a really good magazine. It has a lot of different information and I like the way it is set up.

The most important thing I learned was take care of your environment while you still have it, and many things affect the environment. I like how it talks about the scientists and their experiences.

I learned that there is a lot more rural area than nonrural.

I learned that climate changes may affect human health.

When we see bolded words we should be able to know what the definition is by giving us a definition down below so we don't have to use the glossary as much and lose our place.

I learned how carbon is deposited through the Earth.

Explain what carbon dioxide does to our bodies.

You could make it a little more fun and not so boring.

About *Natural IQ*

Scientists report their research in journals, which are special booklets that enable scientists to share information with one another. This journal, *Natural IQ*, was created so that scientists can share their research with you and with other middle school students. Each article tells you about scientific research conducted by scientists in the Forest Service, U.S. Department of Agriculture. If you want to know more about the Forest Service, you can read about it on the inside back cover of this journal, or you can visit the *Natural Inquirer* Web site at http://www.naturalinquirer.org. *Natural IQ* is a member of the *Natural Inquirer* family of science journals. *Natural IQ* focuses on a specific U.S. region. This *Natural IQ* describes research in the Southern United States.

All of the research in *Natural IQ* is concerned with nature, such as trees, forests, animals, insects, outdoor activities, and water. First, you will "Meet the Scientists" who conducted the research. Then you will read something special about science and about the natural environment. You will also read about a specific research project, which is written in the format that scientists use when they publish their research in journals. Then, YOU will become the scientist when you conduct the FACTivity associated with each article. Don't forget to look at the glossary and the special sections highlighted in each article.

At the end of each section of the article, you will find a few questions to help you think about what you have read. Your teacher may use these questions in a class discussion.

Who Are Scientists?

Scientists are people who collect and evaluate information about a wide range of topics. Some scientists study the natural environment. To be a successful scientist, you must:

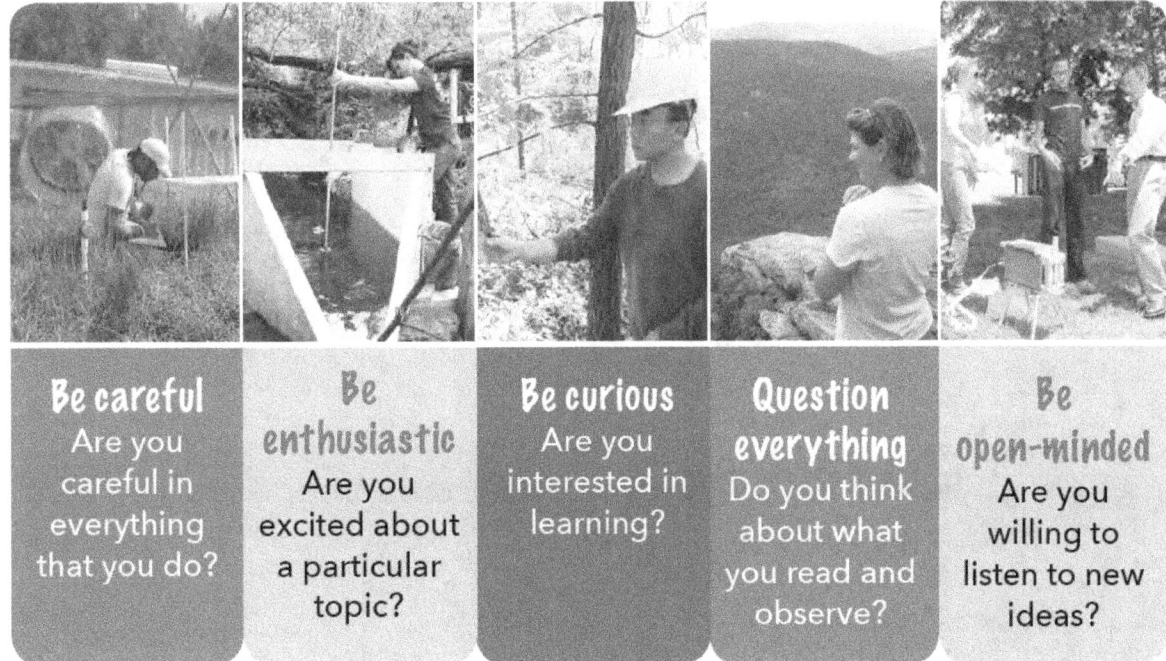

Be careful
Are you careful in everything that you do?

Be enthusiastic
Are you excited about a particular topic?

Be curious
Are you interested in learning?

Question everything
Do you think about what you read and observe?

Be open-minded
Are you willing to listen to new ideas?

Welcome to the Southern United States Climate Change Edition of *Natural IQ!*

GLOSSARY WORDS ARE IN **BOLD** AND DEFINED ON PAGE 8.

Over the past 100 years, the global climate has been changing. In the event of continued climate change, forests of the future likely will be different from the forests of today. Forest managers must manage forests even as the forests change.

The element carbon plays an important role in climate change. All living and once-living things contain carbon. About half of the weight of a tree, if all of its water is removed, is carbon. Living trees hold carbon. When trees are planted and cared for, less carbon is released into the atmosphere. Wood products produced from trees also hold carbon.

One of the main causes of global climate change is an increase in **atmospheric** carbon dioxide. Carbon dioxide is a gaseous form of carbon. Carbon dioxide is released into the atmosphere from many sources (FIG. 1). Forest managers can help to reduce the amount of carbon dioxide released into the atmosphere. Forest managers reduce atmospheric carbon dioxide when they plant and care for trees.

Forests and other types of land provide benefits to people. Some of these benefits include clean air, clean water, wildlife **habitat**, food, scenery, and places to **recreate**. These kinds of benefits are called **ecosystem** benefits. Another ecosystem benefit is that forests help to slow the rate of climate change. As the climate changes and forests change, the ecosystem benefits may change as well. Forest managers want to preserve as many ecosystem benefits as possible as forests change.

The Forest Service, U.S. Department of Agriculture, has scientists who are helping forest managers preserve ecosystem benefits.

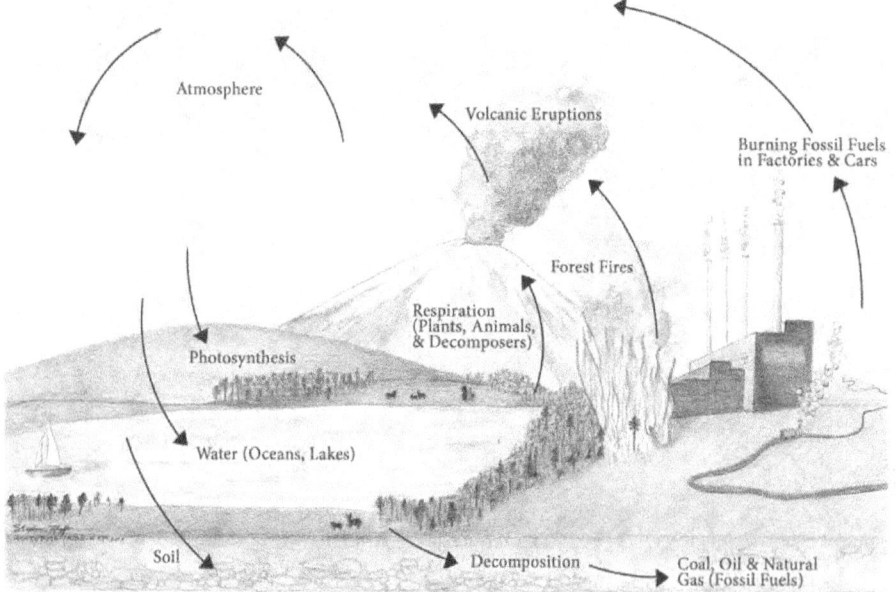

FIGURE 1. THE CARBON CYCLE. CARBON IS CYCLED FROM THE ATMOSPHERE TO EARTH AND THEN BACK AGAIN INTO THE ATMOSPHERE. ILLUSTRATION BY STEPHANIE PFEIFFER.

Some Forest Service scientists, whose research you will read about in this journal, study our changing climate and forests. These scientists focus their research on two areas. First, these Forest Service scientists explore ways to adapt to the changing climate and changing forests. Second, Forest Service scientists explore ways to better understand how trees hold carbon. This includes studying how to manage trees so that more carbon is held on Earth's surface. This second area of research is called **mitigation**.

Forests in the Southern United States

Almost 30 percent of forest land in the United States is found in 13 Southern States (FIG. 2). The future of forests in the South is affected by at least four things:

1. Population growth

2. Climate change

3. The demand for wood products

4. **Invasive species**

Another important factor in the future of southern forests is land development, or **urbanization**. Increasing urbanization will mean that more carbon will be released

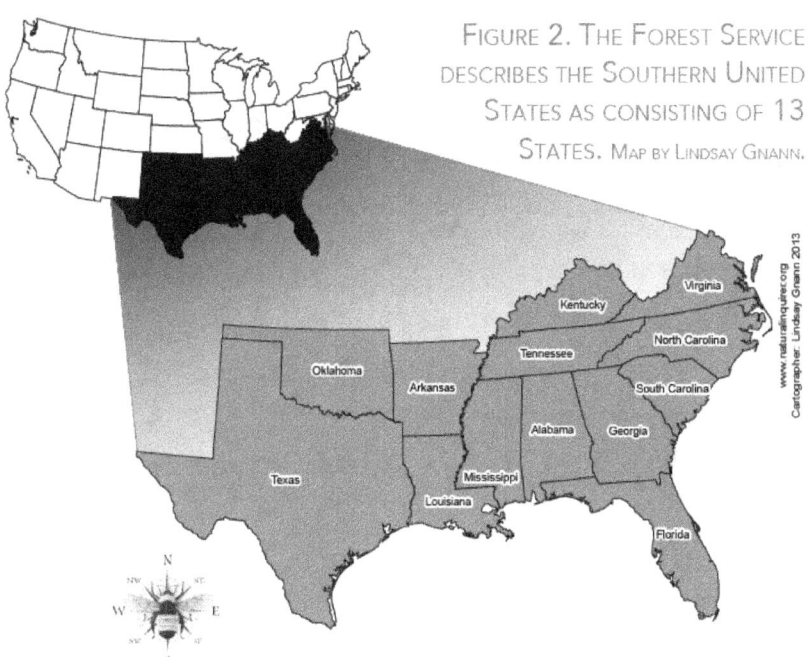

FIGURE 2. THE FOREST SERVICE DESCRIBES THE SOUTHERN UNITED STATES AS CONSISTING OF 13 STATES. MAP BY LINDSAY GNANN.

into the atmosphere. More carbon will be released because forests will be removed to build roads and structures. Another reason for increased atmospheric carbon is that more people create more **fossil fuel emissions**. These emissions are one of the main causes of increasing atmospheric carbon dioxide levels.

In the Southern United States, climate change is expected to bring additional changes. Globally, average temperatures are predicted to rise between 2 and 6 degrees Celsius (°C) by the year 2100. **Precipitation** patterns are expected to change also. The number and **duration** of dry periods are expected to increase. Rising temperatures and different precipitation patterns will change southern forests.

Forest Service scientists are interested in learning how southern forests will change as the climate changes. These

What Do the Abbreviations F and C Stand For?

F is the abbreviation that stands for Fahrenheit, a nonmetric temperature scale, and C is the abbreviation for Celsius, the metric temperature scale. The ° symbol stands for "degrees." So, "18 °C" is read as "eighteen degrees Celsius." You will see temperatures written this way in *Natural IQ* articles as well as in articles that scientists publish in other journals. Most scientific publications use the metric scale.

scientists are interested in learning how we can adapt to our changing climate and forests. Scientists want to learn about how southern forests can help slow climate change by holding more carbon on Earth.

You will read about five scientific studies in this journal. All of the studies are concerned with climate change. In one article, you will learn whether the 13 Southern States have held or released more carbon into the atmosphere over the last 100 years. In another article, you will think about what will happen to streams when different **species** of trees are planted close to them. Another article will help you discover whether scientists are predicting more or fewer wildfires in the South's future. You will learn how southern **rural** areas are likely to be affected by the changing climate. Finally, you will discover what scientists are learning about where nonnative plant and animal species are likely to live in the future. Nonnative means that the plant or animal species does not naturally live in the area. As you read these articles, you will discover how climate change is affecting the South's land, wildlife, air, water, and wildland fires.

Glossary

atmospheric (at mə **sfēr** ik): Of, relating to, or occurring in the atmosphere. The atmosphere is the whole mass of air surrounding Earth.

duration (du **rā** shən): The time during which something exists or lasts.

ecosystem (**ē** kō **sis** təm): Community of plants and animal species interacting with one another and with the nonliving environment.

fossil fuel emission (**fä** səl **fyü(-ə)l** ē **mi** shən): The discharge or sending out of fossil fuels. Fossil fuels are fuels, such as coal, petroleum, or natural gas, formed from the fossilized remains of plants and animals.

habitat (**ha** bə tat): The place or environment where a plant or animal naturally or normally lives and grows.

invasive species (in **vā** siv **spē** shēz): Any plant, animal, or organism that is not native to the ecosystem it is in, and is likely to cause harm to the environment, the economy, or human health. All invasive species are nonnative species, but many nonnative species are not invasive species because they do not cause harm.

mitigation (**mi** tə **gā** shən): Action taken to cause something to be less harsh, hostile, or severe.

precipitation (pri **si** pə **tā** shən): Rain, hail, snow, mist, or sleet.

recreate (**re** krē āt): To take recreation; to enjoy leisure time.

rural (**rür** əl): Outside of the city.

species (**spē** shēz): A class of individuals having common attributes and designated by a common name.

urbanization (**ər** bə nə **zā** shən): The process by which towns and cities are formed and become larger as more and more people begin living and working in central areas.

Accented syllables are in **bold**. Definitions and marks are from http://www.merriam-webster.com.

Everything but the Carbon Sink:

Carbon Storage in the Southern United States

Photo by Babs McDonald.

What Kinds of Scientists Did This Research?

plant ecologist: This scientist studies the relationship of plants with one another and with other organisms in the environment.

plant pathologist: This scientist studies plant diseases.

systems ecologist: This scientist studies the way an ecosystem functions as a whole. An ecosystem is a community of plant and animal species interacting with one another and with the nonliving environment.

systems modeler: This scientist uses an understanding of relationships to construct models illustrating those relationships. Models are simple versions of more complex things. Some examples are model cars or airplanes. Models can also be built with mathematics, words, and maps.

Thinking About Science

Environmental scientists are interested in how the natural environment works. The natural environment includes all of the living and nonliving things found naturally in an area. Some of these scientists are interested in how the natural environment responds to change. In this research, scientists wondered about change occurring over a span of more than 100 years. To study this change, the scientists used data that had been collected over that many years.

The scientists entered the data into a computer program called a model. The computer model included mathematical equations. The scientists observed changes recorded over a 100-year period. They then developed equations based on the recorded changes. For example, a scientist may observe that the water level in a forest stream drops 1.10 centimeters for every 2 weeks without rain. With this knowledge, the scientist can create an equation that will predict the stream's water level for any number of weeks without rain.

In this research, the scientists were interested in whether an area of land and forests absorbed more carbon than it released into the atmosphere. With the use of a computer model, the scientists were able to identify a pattern over more than 100 years.

▶ How many inches is 1.10 centimeters? Multiply 1.10 by 0.3937 to find out.

Thinking About the Environment

All living and once-living matter contains the element carbon. Think about your own body. A human body contains about 18 percent carbon. The carbon in plants is produced from **atmospheric** carbon dioxide through **photosynthesis**. Plants, therefore, are called producers. Humans get their carbon from eating plants and from eating animals that eat plants. Animals, including humans, are called consumers. A plant contains carbon as long as it lives, and until it completely decays or is burned. Soil and water bodies also contain carbon.

GLOSSARY WORDS ARE IN **BOLD** AND DEFINED ON PAGE 21.

Carbon is held by plants, soil, and water bodies, but some carbon is also released back into the atmosphere. Carbon dioxide, therefore, continually cycles between the atmosphere and Earth (FIG. 1). This exchange occurs in the form of carbon dioxide. A carbon source is when more carbon is released by the environment than is produced through photosynthesis. A carbon sink is when more carbon is produced through photosynthesis than is released to the atmosphere.

FIGURE 1.
THE CARBON CYCLE.
ILLUSTRATION BY STEPHANIE PFEIFFER.

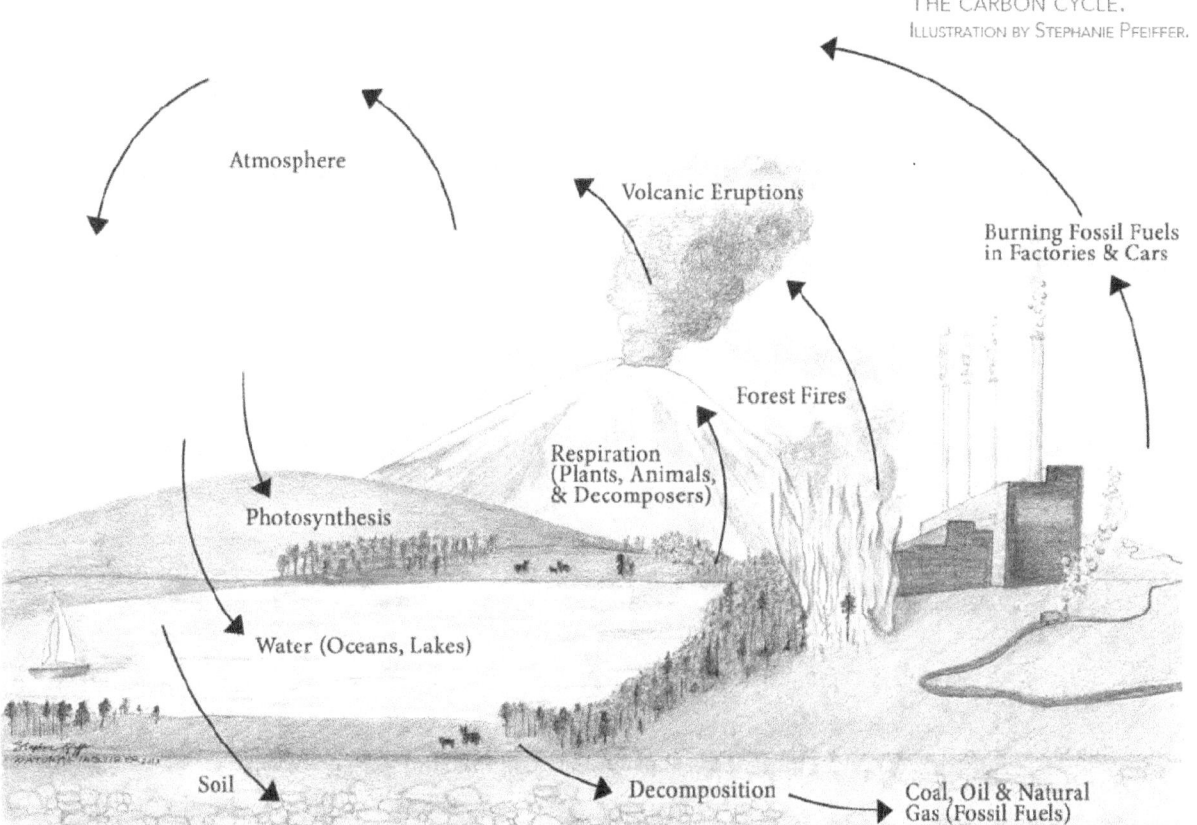

Atmosphere

Volcanic Eruptions

Burning Fossil Fuels in Factories & Cars

Forest Fires

Respiration (Plants, Animals, & Decomposers)

Photosynthesis

Water (Oceans, Lakes)

Soil

Decomposition

Coal, Oil & Natural Gas (Fossil Fuels)

Introduction

The scientists in this study were interested in environmental changes occurring in the Southern United States (FIG. 2). The scientists were interested in changes occurring over a long time. In particular, the scientists were interested in the following environmental changes:

- Increasing atmospheric carbon dioxide

- Increasing ozone

- Increasing nitrogen on Earth

- Climate change (Climate change is the long-term change in global weather patterns, especially increases in temperature, storm activity, and **precipitation**)

- Changes in land use (FIG. 3)

FIGURE 2. THE FOREST SERVICE DESCRIBES THE SOUTHERN UNITED STATES AS CONSISTING OF 13 STATES. MAP BY LINDSAY GNANN.

FIGURE 3. LAND USE IS THE TYPE OF COVER THAT IS FOUND ON ANY GIVEN PART OF EARTH'S SURFACE. LAND USE EXAMPLES INCLUDE FORESTS, FARMS, SHOPPING CENTERS, CITIES, HOMES, ROADS, AND WATER BODIES. WOULD YOU CALL YOUR SCHOOLYARD OR BACKYARD A TYPE OF LAND USE? WHY?

The scientists were interested in how these five changes will affect the carbon cycle of the Southern United States (SEE FIG. 1).

Carbon dioxide continually cycles between Earth and the atmosphere. In the past, this cycling created an average balance over time between atmospheric carbon dioxide and carbon on Earth. Over the past 100 years, however, human activities have increased the amount of carbon dioxide released to the atmosphere. Carbon dioxide is released when trees are removed for development (FIG. 4) and when **fossil fuels** are burned for energy.

Human activities have caused other changes. **Tropospheric** ozone, another gas, helps protect Earth from the Sun's **ultraviolet radiation** (FIG. 5). When fossil fuels are burned, however, too much ozone is produced near Earth's surface. This ozone contributes to creating a kind of air pollution called smog.

FIGURE 4. WHEN TREES ARE REMOVED AND BURNED TO MAKE ROOM FOR URBAN DEVELOPMENT, THE CARBON IN THE TREES IS RELEASED INTO THE ATMOSPHERE. IN THIS EXAMPLE, THE CARBON BALANCE AND LAND USE ARE AFFECTED. BESIDES TREE REMOVAL, IDENTIFY ONE MORE SOURCE OF ATMOSPHERIC CARBON DIOXIDE IN THIS PHOTO.

PHOTOS BY BABS MCDONALD.

Meet the Scientist

Dafeng Hui,
PLANT ECOLOGIST:

My favorite science experience is working with students to collect experimental data in the field. It is always a pleasure to **stimulate** students' interests and bring new students to this research area. When students work on real-world issues, they learn quickly and better understand the problem. We also had the opportunity to observe closely and learn more about the natural world. In this photo, I am on the right. I am showing research equipment to university students Chloe Davidson and Robert Johnson. This research equipment measures photosynthesis.

Another long-term change involves nitrogen. Human activities have caused an increase in nitrogen on Earth's surface. Nitrogen is released when fossil fuels are burned for energy. Much of this nitrogen returns to Earth. Nitrogen is also used as a crop fertilizer. Over time or in large amounts, nitrogen adds too much acid to plants, soil, and water bodies. In the short term or in smaller amounts, nitrogen can cause an increase in plant growth. This growth occurs because the plants are able to use nitrogen as a **nutrient**.

The scientists were interested in land use changes over the past 100 years. Over time, for example, forests have been cut and regrown. Farms have been **cultivated** and abandoned. Land developed for buildings and roads is one type of land use change that is not usually reversed (FIG. 6).

FIGURE 5. THE ATMOSPHERE'S LEVELS. IN WHICH LEVEL IS OZONE FOUND? ILLUSTRATION BY NICKOLA DUDLEY.

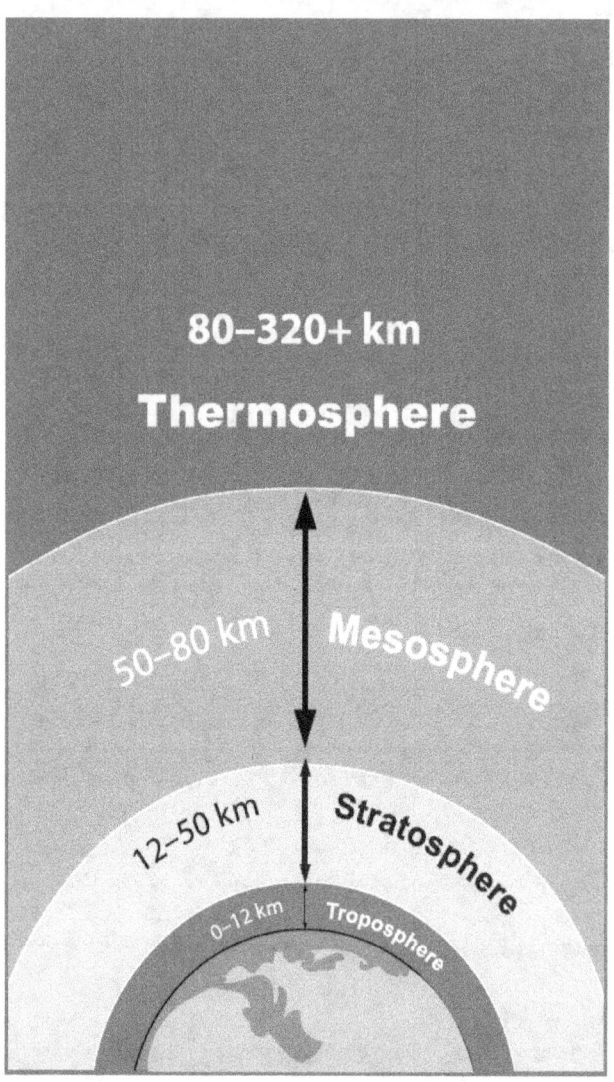

80–320+ km

Thermosphere

50–80 km Mesosphere

12–50 km Stratosphere

0–12 km Troposphere

FIGURE 6. SOME KINDS OF LAND USES ARE MORE EASILY CHANGED THAN OTHERS.

PHOTOS BY BABS MCDONALD.

The scientists were also interested in the changing climate. Over the past 100 years, the average yearly temperature has been rising around the world. This average rising temperature may have an effect, for example, on where and how much rain falls.

The scientists in this study wanted to know how these environmental changes have affected how land in the Southern United States holds carbon or releases it to the atmosphere. The scientists wondered if the Southern United States has been a carbon source or a carbon sink over the past 100 years. A carbon source is when more carbon is released by the environment than is produced through photosynthesis. A carbon sink is when more carbon is produced through photosynthesis than is released to the atmosphere.

Reflection Section

 What was the question the scientists wanted to answer? Be specific about what the scientists were studying.

 What is one of the primary reasons for many of the changes studied by the scientists in this study?

What Is Net Carbon Exchange?

A carbon sink or carbon source is measured by the amount of carbon absorbed or released over a period of time. The measurement does not include the carbon already present in the plant, soil, or water body.

Think about your own body. Each time you take a breath, you breathe in an amount of oxygen. You also expel an amount of carbon dioxide. Your body, however, contains additional amounts of each gas. The **volume** of oxygen coming in could be compared with the volume of carbon dioxide going out.

Scientists compare the amount of carbon dioxide absorbed in an area with the amount being released. Any excess amount determines whether an area is a carbon sink or source. Scientists measure the excess quantity over time. This quantity is called net carbon exchange or NCE. A positive NCE value indicates a carbon sink. A negative NCE value indicates a carbon source. By measuring NCE, scientists observe and record changes in carbon storage over time.

Methods

The scientists were interested in studying environmental changes that have occurred over the past 100 years. They used data that were collected between 1895 and 2007 across the Southern United States (FIG. 7).

The scientists divided the Southern United States into a grid of blocks 8 kilometers by 8 kilometers in size (FIG. 8). A value for each **variable** in figure 7 was calculated and assigned to each block.

FIGURE 7. THE SCIENTISTS USED THE FOLLOWING DATA THAT WERE COLLECTED BY OTHER SCIENTISTS BETWEEN 1895 AND 2007. THESE DATA ARE CALLED VARIABLES, BECAUSE THEIR VALUE CAN CHANGE OR VARY.

The amount of carbon dioxide in the atmosphere
The amount of ozone in the atmosphere
The amount of nitrogen fertilizer being used for agriculture
The amount of acid in the soil
The amount of nitrogen released on Earth's surface through burning fossil fuels
The average yearly temperature
Minimum and maximum yearly temperatures
The amount of yearly rainfall and snowfall
The amount of land in acres in various land use categories in certain years, including forests, farmland, and urban land
Net Carbon Exchange (NCE, for short): This is a measure of the amount of carbon produced through photosynthesis, minus the amount of carbon dioxide released into the atmosphere from various sources.

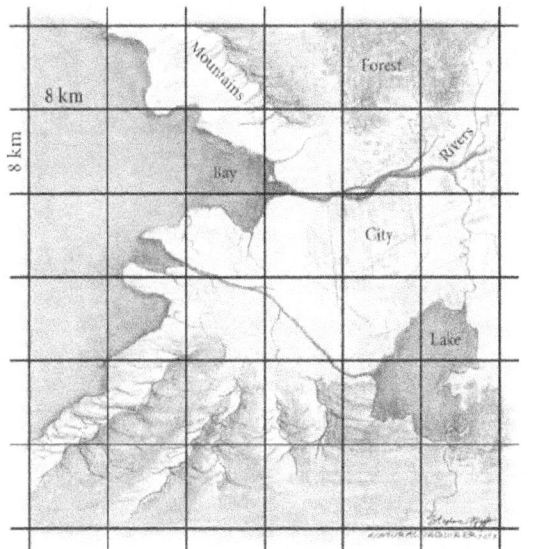

FIGURE 8. THE ENTIRE SOUTHERN UNITED STATES WAS DIVIDED INTO A GRID OF BLOCKS 8 KILOMETERS LONG ON A SIDE. THIS EXAMPLE SHOWS A LAND AREA DIVIDED INTO A GRID.

ILLUSTRATION BY STEPHANIE PFEIFFER AND LINDSAY GNANN.

The scientists entered all of the data into a computer. The scientists developed a computer program, called a model, to **analyze** the data. The model used equations to calculate NCE. The scientists then compared all combinations of variables in figure 7 with the value NCE. This process was done for each block in the grid over the entire 112 years. Then all of the data in all blocks were averaged to produce values for the entire Southern United States.

Number Crunches

▶ How many years of data did the scientists gather?

▶ How many miles across is the side of each block in the grid? Multiply the number of kilometers by 0.62 to find out.

▶ How many square kilometers are contained in each block?

▶ How many square miles are contained in each block?

Reflection Section

⇨ What is one advantage of using data collected by another scientist?

⇨ What is one disadvantage of using data collected by another scientist?

⇨ Explain NCE in your own words. What would an NCE value of 0 mean?

⇨ Which is more desirable in today's world: A carbon sink or a carbon source?

Number Crunch
work area

Findings

The findings in figure 9 show values for NCE in the Southern United States over three time periods.

FIGURE 9. NET CARBON EXCHANGE (NCE) IN THE SOUTHERN UNITED STATES FROM 1895 TO 2007. A NEGATIVE VALUE INDICATES A CARBON SOURCE.

	Percent change	NCE in petagrams
1895 → 1951	4.11	-1.20
1951 → 2007	7.12	2.00
1895 → 2007	2.72	0.80

Number Crunches

▶ What percentage of the world's **terrestrial** carbon is stored by plants and soil in the Southern United States? Divide 26 by 653 to find out.

▶ How many elephants would equal the weight of all of the carbon held in the plants and soil of the Southern United States? Multiply 26 Pg by 25,000 elephants to find out.

The Southern United States was a carbon sink for the period of 1895–2007, over which there was an increase in terrestrial carbon of 0.80 Pg (SEE FIG. 9). This amount accounted for 2.7 percent of the total carbon stored across the entire Southern United States in 1895. Between 1895 and 1950, however, the Southern United States was a carbon source of 1.20 Pg. Between 1951 and 2007, the Southern United States was again a carbon sink, storing an additional 2.0 Pg of carbon. The scientists believe that the Southern United States was a carbon source

Science Fun Fact:

What Is a Petagram?

A petagram (Pg) is a unit of measurement. A Pg is equal to 10^{15} grams, which is 10x10x10x10x10x10x 10x10x10x10x10x10 x10x10x10, which is 1,000,000,000,000,000 grams, or one quintillion grams. One Pg of carbon is equal to the weight of 25,000 elephants.

The scientists in this study estimated the amount of carbon stored in the Southern United States' plants and soil. Their estimate of total storage was 26 Pg of carbon. According to the United Nations Food and Agriculture Organization, trees store 289 Pg of carbon worldwide. The world's trees, soil, and **leaf litter** store an estimated 653 Pg of carbon.

Photos by Babs McDonald.

FIGURE 10. WHICH LAND USE STORES THE MOST AMOUNT OF CARBON?

between 1895 and 1951 because many acres of forest land were cleared for agriculture. From the 1950s until the late 1900s, many of these agricultural lands were abandoned and forests grew back.

Overall, the scientists found that changes in land uses over the past 112 years have had a negative impact on carbon storage in the Southern United States. The scientists discovered that different kinds of land use stored different amounts of carbon (FIG. 10). The application of nitrogen fertilizer and an increase in nitrogen released on Earth had a positive impact on carbon storage. This positive impact is from the beneficial effects of nitrogen on plant growth. When plants grow, more carbon is stored.

Climate change, as an individual variable, appeared to have little direct impact on carbon storage in the Southern United States. However, when considering that most of the other variables studied had an impact on climate change, some of the change in carbon storage can be **indirectly** related to climate change.

Although the Southern United States was a carbon sink over the past 112 years, many factors influenced carbon storage positively and negatively. Some factors related to climate change had a negative effect, for example, but were **offset** by increased nitrogen and the application of nitrogen fertilizer. Land use change had a negative effect, but was offset by an increase in the amount of forest land in the Southern United States.

Reflection Section
Reflection Section

 Land use in the Southern United States is changing, with more land developed for homes, shopping centers, roads, and office parks. If this trend continues, do you think the Southern United States will remain a carbon sink or will it once again become a carbon source? Why?

 Think about the finding that even though the Southern United States was a carbon sink over the past 112 years, many factors influenced carbon storage positively and negatively over this time period. This finding highlights that scientists do not always get absolute answers to their questions. Pretend that you are one of the scientists on this study. How would you explain to the press the importance of discovering that both positive and negative factors influence carbon storage?

Discussion

The scientists found that an increase in atmospheric carbon dioxide and nitrogen created a carbon sink over the time period. Increases in ground-level ozone, urban development, and a changing climate contributed most to carbon losses.

The scientists noted that the list of variables they considered was incomplete. Forest management, for example, could affect NCE but was not included in the model. Hurricanes, fires, and other natural disturbances were also not included in the model. If these variables were included, NCE estimates might be different.

The scientists said that additional research is needed to better understand how changes on the planet contribute to the carbon balance between Earth and the atmosphere.

Reflection Section

Reflection Section

⇨ How might an increase in atmospheric carbon dioxide help create a carbon sink?

⇨ What is the paradox of an increase in atmospheric carbon dioxide helping to create a carbon sink? A paradox is a situation that is unexpected because it defies logic or reason.

⇨ Why is it important to understand how human-caused changes contribute to NCE?

Adapted from Tian, H., Chen, G., Zhang, C. [and others]. 2012. Century-scale responses of ecosystem carbon storage and flux to multiple environmental changes in the Southern United States. Ecosystems. 15: 674-694. http://www.srs.fs.fed.us/pubs/ja/2012/ja_2012_tian_002.pdf

PHOTOS BY BARB McDONALD.

Glossary

analyze (**a** nə līz): To study or examine carefully.

atmospheric (at mə **sfēr** ik): Of, relating to, or occurring in the atmosphere. The atmosphere is the whole mass of air surrounding Earth.

biomass (**bī** ō mas): Living matter.

consumer (kən **sü** mər): A person or thing that consumes or uses something. In this case, consumers are animals that eat plants and other animals.

cultivate (**kəl** tə vāt): Prepare for planting.

fossil fuel (**fä** səl **fyü(-ə)**l): Fuel, such as coal, petroleum, or natural gas, formed from the fossilized remains of plants and animals.

indirect (**in** dī rekt): Not straightforward and open; not directly aimed at.

leaf litter (**lēf li** tər): The top layer of dead and decaying leaves, small sticks, and twigs that lay on the forest floor.

nutrient (**nü** trē ənt): A substance that plants, animals, and people need to live and grow.

offset (of **set**): To serve as a counterbalance for or to compensate for.

photosynthesis (**fō** tō **sin(t)** thə səs): The process by which green plants use sunlight to form sugars and starches from water and carbon dioxide.

precipitation (pri **si** pə **tā** shən): Rain, hail, snow, mist, or sleet.

producer (prō **dü** sər): An organism (such as a green plant) viewed as a source of living matter that can be consumed by other organisms.

stimulate (**stim** ü lāt): To excite to activity, greater activity, or growth.

terrestrial (tə **res** t(r)ē əl): Of or relating to land as opposed to air or water.

tropospheric (trō pə **sfēr** ik): Of or relating to the part of the atmosphere, measured from the surface of the planet to about 6 miles.

ultraviolet radiation (**əl** trə **vī** (ə-)lət **rā** dē **ā** shən): Light waves located beyond the visible spectrum at its violet end and having a wavelength shorter than those of visible light but longer than those of X-rays.

variable (**ver** ē ə bəl): Something that is able or apt to vary.

volume (**väl** yüm): The amount of a substance.

FACTivity

Time Needed
30-40 minutes

Materials
- Photo sheets and answer sheets provided in this FACTivity
- Pencil
- Blank paper or science notebook (optional)

In this research, you learned about carbon sinks and carbon sources. You learned about different land uses and whether they are more likely to be a carbon sink or source. The questions you will answer in this FACTivity are: What are the characteristics of an area identified as a carbon sink? What are the characteristics of an area identified as a carbon source?

Methods

You may work individually, in pairs, or in small groups. Examine the two photo sheets provided in the next section. Identify whether you believe each photo shows an area that is a carbon sink or a carbon source. Your teacher may make copies of the answer sheet, or you may use the one in this journal.

On the answer sheet, indicate whether each photo is a carbon sink or a carbon source. Then, explain what makes the area a sink or a source by writing one or two complete sentences. Recall that a carbon sink is an area that absorbs more carbon through photosynthesis than it releases. A carbon source is an area that releases more carbon than it absorbs through photosynthesis. Then, rank all of the photos from one to eight. Rank the photos from the most powerful carbon sink to the most powerful carbon source.

On your own, write a short paragraph describing the main characteristics of a carbon sink. Write a short paragraph describing the main characteristics of a carbon source. These paragraphs should be based on your photo observations and evaluations. Use complete sentences with proper grammar and punctuation.

Your teacher will lead a class discussion about what makes an area a carbon sink or a carbon source. As a class, discuss your rankings. Did everyone agree and if not, why not? As a class, determine whether the area around your school is a carbon sink or source. To do this, your class must first agree on how large an area you will consider. Then, identify three opportunities to improve the area's status as a carbon sink. Write these three ideas in complete sentences and develop a plan to implement them in the area around your school.

Carbon sink or carbon source?

1

2

PHOTOS BY BABS MCDONALD.

3

4

Carbon sink or carbon source?

5

6

PHOTOS BY BABS McDONALD.

7

8

NOTE: 1 is most powerful carbon sink, 8 is the most powerful carbon source.

Photo	Carbon sink or source?	Why is this area a carbon sink or a carbon source? (1–2 sentences)	Rank order from 1-8
1			
2			
3			
4			
5			
6			
7			
8			

Describe the obvious visual characteristics of a carbon sink.	Describe the obvious visual characteristics of a carbon source.	Three ways to improve our schoolyard's status as a carbon sink are:

FACTivity Extension

To complete this extension, you must have either a smartphone or a digital camera. Using your smartphone or camera, take five photos of areas around your community that are carbon sinks. Take five photos that are carbon sources. Share your photos with the class and describe why you think the area is a carbon sink or source. As a class, identify ways to move the carbon source areas toward carbon sinks.

Web Resources

A Student's Guide to Global Climate Change by the U.S. Environmental Protection Agency
http://www.epa.gov/climatestudents/

Climate Kids: NASA's Eyes on the Earth
http://climatekids.nasa.gov/

NOAA Climate Change for Students
http://www.education.noaa.gov/Climate/

Pachamama: Our Earth--Our Future
http://www.grida.no/publications/other/geo2000/pacha/

U.S. Environmental Protection Agency Ozone Web site
http://www.epa.gov/glo/

An Article about Fossil Fuels and the Nitrogen Cycle
http://news.mongabay.com/2009/0604-hance_nitrogen.html

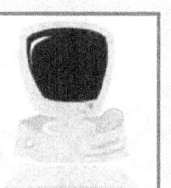

✳ "Everything but the Carbon Sink" is taken from the saying "Everything but the kitchen sink." This saying means that nearly everything possible is being included, usually when someone is taking items from a place.

If you are a trained Project Learning Tree-educator, you may use *Our Changing Climate* or *Our Changing World* as additional resources.

Flow Down!

Can Managing Forests Help Maintain Water Supplies in the Face of Climate Change?

What Kinds of Scientists Did This Research?

ecologist: This scientist studies the relationship of living things with their living and nonliving environment.

hydrologist: This scientist studies water and water systems.

PHOTO COURTESY OF U.S. FOREST SERVICE.

Stephanie Laseter, HYDROLOGIST:

A favorite recent experience of mine was installing a series of flumes in several stream channels. We can use these flumes to measure the amount of water flowing in the streams. Installing these instruments means that we get to hike through the forest in search of the perfect location in the stream. In this photo, I am standing by a flume.

Once a site is chosen, we fit a large fiberglass flume into the stream channel, making sure that we have it perfectly level. We can use an instrument called a pressure transducer to measure the height of the water in the flume. By putting these flumes in sites that have different forest types and various forest ages, we can learn a lot about how these forests use and store water.

Thinking About Science

Sometimes when scientists conduct their research, they collect data over a short period of time and then they analyze the data and draw conclusions. The scientists use data from shorter time periods because those data are usually the most accessible. Obtaining data that span decades is often difficult because of the money and other resources needed to obtain data over a long time period. However, when data are available over long time periods, scientists are thrilled to use it. Scientists like to use these data because these data offer the opportunity to discover long-term trends as opposed to only having short snapshots of how a system is responding.

Think about if someone has a bad year in school and they are evaluated on just this one year for getting into college. Do you think it is better to look at one year or several years the student was in school to make a decision about getting into college? Looking at several years a student has been in school is a better way of determining whether to accept a person into college. It is a better way because it provides more details and history about the person. Similarly, this longer-term understanding provides scientists with more detail for them to draw their conclusions. In this study, the scientists analyzed **streamflow** data over a 75-year time period.

Thinking About the Environment

Have you ever heard the term "ecosystem services?" Ecosystem services are provided by healthy natural areas just because they are healthy natural areas. Examples include clean air, clean water, beautiful landscapes, healthy soil, places for wildlife to live, minerals, and even places to do outdoor activities. Ecosystem services are important because they provide goods and services that are vital to human health and quality of life. For example, many people rely on water from streams for drinking water and everyday use in their homes.

Ecosystem services can be influenced by many things. For example, climate change can influence ecosystem services because landscapes and ecosystems may change how they function or look due to the change in climate. In this study, the scientists were interested in ecosystem services, including streamflow, provided by forested **watersheds**. The scientists were interested in how climate change may impact the streamflow provided by these forests (FIG. 1).

FIGURE 1. A WATERSHED IS AN AREA OF LAND WHERE ALL OF THE WATER THAT IS UNDERGROUND WITHIN THE AREA, AND ALL OF THE WATER IN STREAMS AND RIVERS IN THE AREA, FLOWS TO THE SAME PLACE. ILLUSTRATION BY STEPHANIE PFEIFFER.

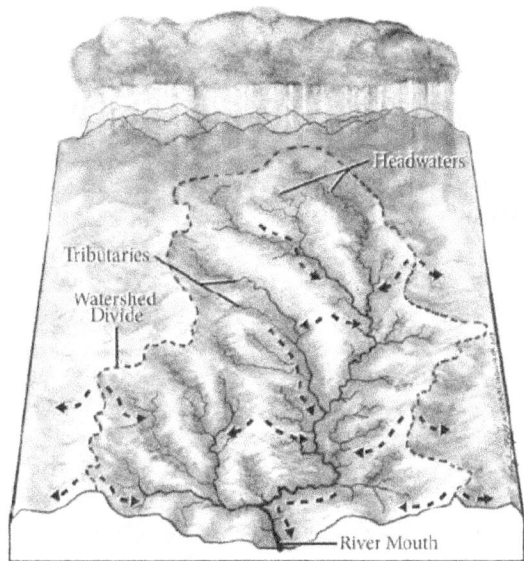

Introduction

Climate change can have direct and indirect impacts on water resources. Direct impacts of climate change can be seen by the presence of more extreme weather events. Extreme weather events include things like heat waves and droughts (FIG. 2). Droughts have a direct impact on water and water supply. The indirect impacts of climate change on water resources relate to temperature and the amount of carbon dioxide in the atmosphere. For example, an increase in temperature could increase the amount of water plants use because of **transpiration** and **evaporation** (FIG. 3). If plants increase their use of water, then there will be less water available for streamflow or **groundwater**.

Forests and how forests are managed also have impacts on water resources. For example, some types of forest management change the number of trees in an area. The number of trees that are in an area influence how much water is **intercepted** by these trees. The number of trees also influences how much water evaporates in this area. Forest management can change the way water flows. Some types of forest management can also create disturbances in the soil. The scientists **hypothesized** that climate impacts may either be made better or worse by forest management that changes the **land cover**.

The scientists in this study wanted to figure out how forest management, climate change, and streamflow interact. First, the scientists wanted to identify if forest management could affect streamflow. Second, the scientists wanted to identify types of forest management that would help protect against extreme precipitation changes that may occur as the climate changes.

FIGURE 2. DROUGHTS CAN HAVE A HUGE IMPACT ON GROWING PLANTS. PHOTO BY R.L. CROISSANT AND COURTESY OF HTTP://WWW.BUGWOOD.ORG.

FIGURE 3. EVAPORATION AND TRANSPIRATION ARE PART OF THE WATER CYCLE. ILLUSTRATION BY STEPHANIE PFEIFFER.

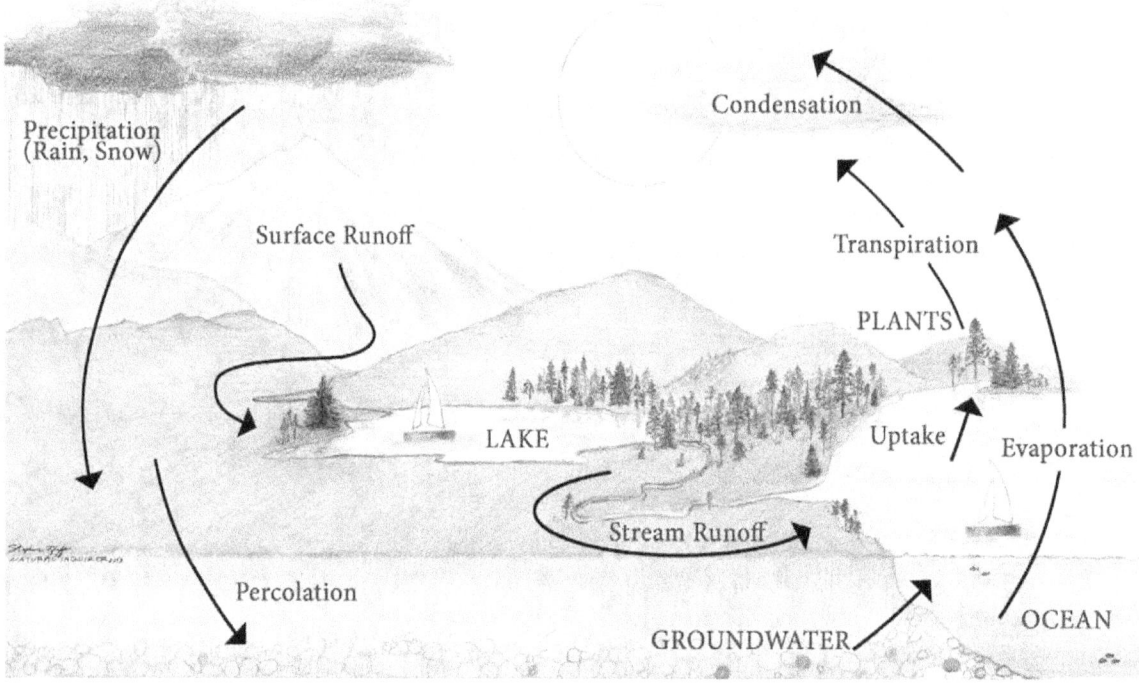

Reflection Section

Reflection Section

 In your own words and in the form of a question, state what questions the scientists were trying to answer.

 Do you think it is important to figure out how forest management, climate change, and streamflow interact? Why or why not?

 Look at figure 3. In this illustration, identify one more way trees and other plants contribute to the water cycle.

Methods

The scientists obtained their data from an area called the Coweeta basin in the Southern Appalachian mountains (FIGS. 4A, 4B, AND 5). Air temperature and precipitation have been recorded at the main climate station there since 1934. Nine recording rain gauges and twelve standard rain gauges are located throughout the basin (FIG. 6). Six of these gauges have been recording since 1936.

Meet the Scientist

James Vose,
RESEARCH ECOLOGIST:

Growing up in a big city, I never realized the important connection between forests and the water that I enjoyed for swimming and fishing. The river where I spent most of my summers began as a small creek in a forest more than two States away! Dr. Stephanie Laseter is with me in this photo.

FIGURE 4A. THE COWEETA BASIN IS LOCATED IN THE SOUTHERN UNITED STATES. MAP BY LINDSAY GNANN.

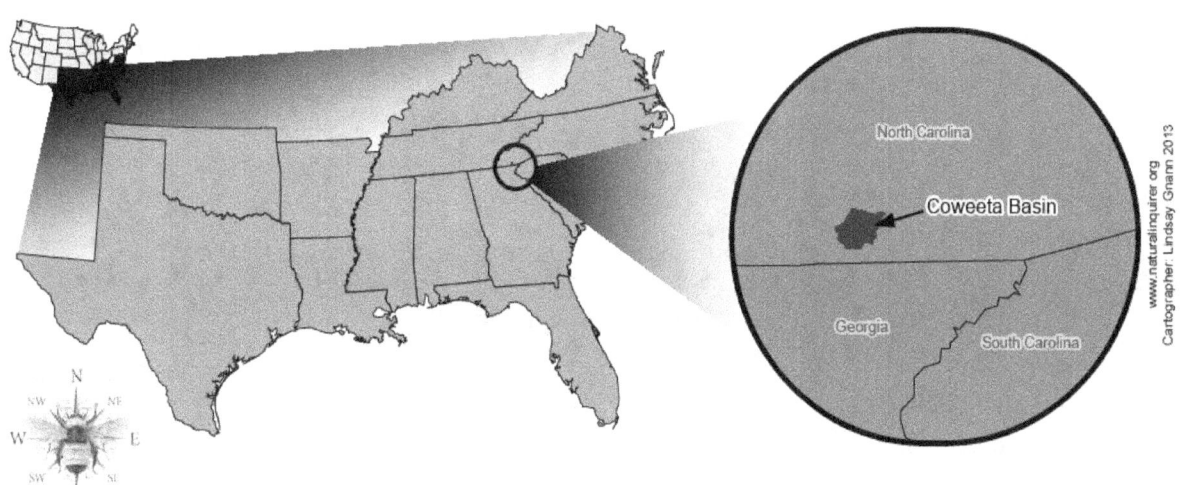

Number Crunch

▶ What percent of the rain gauges have been in use since 1936?

Figure 6. Rain gauges are useful in determining how much and how fast water falls across different areas. The scientists in this study found that the amount of precipitation increased by 30 percent at higher elevations. Why do you think this might happen?

Figure 4b. The Coweeta basin is a forested watershed. Photo courtesy of USDA Forest Service.

Figure 5. The area of study in the Coweeta basin is outlined in the middle of the photo. Photo courtesy of USDA Forest Service.

Photos by Babs McDonald.

The scientists also used long-term streamflow records from six watersheds. The six watersheds had different management and land use histories (FIG. 7).

Watershed (WS=watershed)	Management History
WS1	Changing Tree Types- First, the entire watershed had a **prescribed burn** in 1942. The watershed was changed from Southern Appalachians **deciduous** forest to evergreen, eastern white pine plantation through planting and managing white pine trees.
WS17	Changing Tree Types- First, all woody vegetation was cut in 1941. The watershed was changed from Southern Appalachians deciduous forest to evergreen, eastern white pine plantation through planting and managing white pine trees.
WS37	High-Elevation **Clear-cut**- All woody vegetation cut in 1963.
WS7	Low-Elevation Clear-cut in 1977 and 1978.
WS13	Change to **Coppice** Stand- Clear-cut in 1939-40 and 1962. Vegetation recovered through stump sprouting and existing roots creating a coppice stand.
WS6	Change from Trees to **Successional Vegetation**- Mixed-hardwood forest clear-cut in 1958. Changed to successional vegetation (FIG. 8).

FIGURE 7. EACH WATERSHED HAD A DIFFERENT MANAGEMENT HISTORY.

FIGURE 8. LOOK AT HOW THE TYPE OF VEGETATION CHANGES OVER TIME. WHAT DO YOU NOTICE ABOUT HOW IT CHANGES? ILLUSTRATION BY STEPHANIE PFEIFFER.

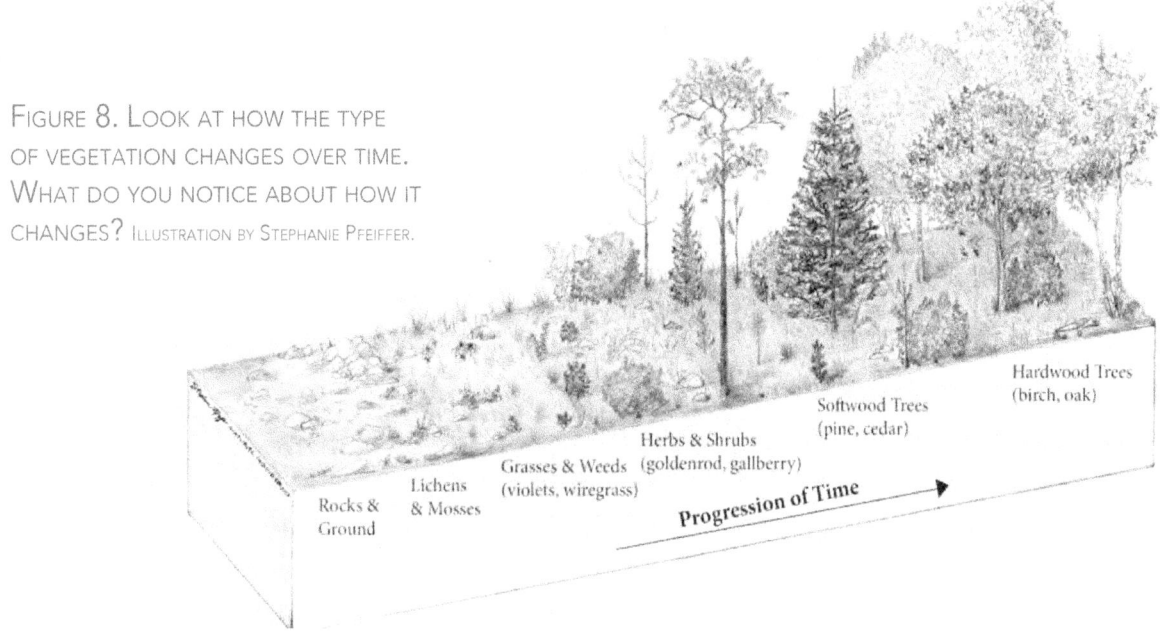

Rocks & Ground

Lichens & Mosses

Grasses & Weeds (violets, wiregrass)

Herbs & Shrubs (goldenrod, gallberry)

Softwood Trees (pine, cedar)

Hardwood Trees (birch, oak)

Progression of Time

What Is a Reference Watershed?

A reference watershed is similar in size, character, and shape to another watershed being studied. The difference between the two watersheds in this study is that people did not take management action on the reference watershed. In some studies, a reference watershed is similar to the watersheds being studied, except that the effects of human activities are not visible or as visible.

If you are familiar with the concept of a **control** in scientific research, you will better understand reference watersheds. A control is one of the experimental conditions in which nothing is changed by the scientist. A control, like a reference watershed, enables a scientist to compare the results of their experiment (or management action) to a condition in which no action was taken.

The scientists were interested in the effect of the different management practices on these watersheds. The scientists compared closely located watersheds that were similar in size and pre-management land conditions. One watershed served as a reference watershed, and the other watersheds had a management treatment applied (SEE FIG. 7).

The scientists created mathematical models to help them explain the interaction between forest management and changes in climate on streamflow. The scientists used future precipitation and temperature forecasts from general circulation models (GCMs) and management histories to estimate the streamflow up to the year 2050. The scientists determined management forecasts by assuming that in 2009, each watershed was managed as it had been in earlier years.

The scientists then predicted how streamflow from the different watersheds might respond to future extreme precipitation events. Extreme precipitation events include extremely dry, or drought, conditions and extremely wet conditions. The scientists' predictions were based on what happened to these watersheds in the past. Instead of past weather and climate **variables**, however, the scientists used weather forecasted for the area from GCMs.

What Is a General Circulation Model?

A general circulation model is a computer model that allows people to forecast weather and predict future changes in climate. A general circulation model (GCM) can **simulate** the interactions of water, atmosphere, land surfaces, and ice. A GCM is run on computers and the output is interpreted by scientists.

Reflection Section

Reflection Section

➡️ The scientists examined six different watersheds with different types of forest management. Why do you think it was important for the scientists to look at a variety of different types of management?

➡️ The scientists compared two watersheds at a time. In your own words, explain this comparison and why it would be useful for the scientists to use.

What Do the Abbreviations F and C Stand For?

F is the abbreviation that stands for Fahrenheit, a nonmetric temperature scale, and C is the abbreviation for Celsius, the metric temperature scale. The ° symbol stands for "degrees." So, "18 °C" is read as "eighteen degrees Celsius." You will see temperatures written this way in *Natural IQ* articles as well as in articles that scientists publish in other journals. Most scientific publications use the metric scale.

Findings

The **mean** annual air temperature has been increasing at Coweeta. Since 1982, the temperature has been increasing at 0.5 °C per decade.

The scientists identified 10 extreme drought years since 1936. Eight of these extreme drought years have occurred since 1980. The most extreme dry year was 2000. The frequency of extreme wet years did not increase with time. The scientists identified 6 extreme wet years. Three of these extreme wet years occurred in the 1970s. The most extreme wet year was 1989. The summer months are becoming drier over time. The fall months are becoming wetter.

The scientists found that predicted streamflow in different future weather conditions was affected by almost all of the management actions examined. This finding supported the scientists' **hypothesis** that climate impacts may either be made better or worse by forest management that changes land cover. The streamflow in different possible climate conditions depended on what type of management action was taken. Converting areas of deciduous trees to pine trees reduced annual streamflow during both extreme wet and extreme

PHOTOS BY BABS MCDONALD.

dry years. Different tree species absorb different amounts of water through their roots. Different species emit different amounts of water from their leaves during transpiration. Because of these differences between tree species, more or less groundwater may be available to fill streams. The type of tree species being managed, therefore, affects the rate of streamflow during both extreme wet and extreme dry years.

Discussion

The scientists found that both temperature and precipitation changed over the time period they studied the Coweeta basin. The scientists determined that management affected the relationship between precipitation and streamflow.

The scientists also determined that how an area is managed has an impact on streamflow. The change from deciduous trees to pine trees reduced annual streamflow during both extreme wet and extreme dry years. The scientists said that the reduced flow may worsen a drought during extreme dry years. However, the reduced flow may also help reduce flooding during extreme wet years.

In areas where pine trees were managed, the scientists found that there is a higher rate of **evapotranspiration** (ē **vap** ō tran spïr **ā** shən) (ET). Greater ET means that soils have more room to store water during wet years. Using this management treatment would be useful, therefore, in a future climate where precipitation is increasing. If the climate becomes drier in the future, however, then this management treatment would not be a good option.

The scientists are not sure if the forest management actions they studied can reduce the effects of climate change. They found, however, that converting areas from deciduous trees to pine trees helps to reduce the impact of **excessive** precipitation. In a future climate with too much precipitation, therefore, this management action would be helpful.

Reflection Section

 Why do you think it is useful for scientists to figure out how climate change may impact an area before the climate changes?

 Why would converting areas from deciduous trees to pine trees not be a good option if the climate becomes drier in the future?

Adapted from Ford, C.R., Laseter, S. H., Swank, W.T., and Vose, J. M. (2011). Can forest management be used to sustain water-based ecosystem services in the face of climate change? Ecological Applications. 21(6), 2049-2067. http://www.srs.fs.usda.gov/pubs/ja/2011/ja_2011_ford_001.pdf

Pinus strobus
White Pine

ILLUSTRATION BY STEPHANIE PFEIFFER.

Glossary

bicarbonate (bī **kär** bə **nāt**): A type of acid that is developed from carbon.

clear-cut (**klēr** kət): A forestry procedure that removes all of the trees in a stand of timber.

control (kən **trōl**): A control is something used for comparison when checking the results of an experiment.

coppice (**kä** pəs): Forest originating mainly from shoots or root suckers rather than seed.

deciduous (di **si** jə wəs): Plants or trees that shed their leaves every year; not evergreen.

evaporation (i **va** p(ə-) **rā** shən): The process of converting water into vapor or fumes.

evapotranspiration: (i **va** pō **tran** spə **rā** shən): Loss of water from Earth by evaporation from Earth's surface and by transpiration from the leaves of plants.

excessive (ik **se** siv): Going beyond what is usual, proper, necessary, or normal.

groundwater (**graünd wä** tər): Water that sinks into the soil and is stored underground.

hypothesis (hī **pä** thə səs): An unproven idea that is accepted for the time being and is often tested during a scientific study.

hypothesize (hī **pä** thə **sīz**): To make an assumption to test its logical consequences.

intercept (**in** tər **sept**): To stop or interrupt the progress or intended course of something.

land cover (**land kə** vər): The observed cover of Earth's surface, such as vegetation and manmade features.

mean (**mēn**): The average in a set of numbers.

prescribed burn (pri **skrīb**ed **bərn**): Controlled fires used to improve forest habitat.

simulate (**sim** yə lāt): To create the appearance or effect of something for purposes of evaluation.

streamflow (**strēm** flō): The movement of water in streams, rivers, and other channels.

successional vegetation (sək **se** shən əl **ve** jə **tā** shən): Plants, trees, and shrubs that naturally replace other plant life over time.

transpiration (**trans** pə **rā** shən): The process by which plants give off water vapor through the stomata in their leaves. Stomata are a part of a leaf and include a pore and special cells which regulate the size of the pore's opening.

variable (**ver** ē ə bəl): Something that is able or apt to vary.

watershed (**wä** tər **shed**): Land area that delivers water and sediment to a major river via small streams.

> Accented syllables are in **bold**. Marks and definitions are from http://www.merriam-webster.com.

FACTivity

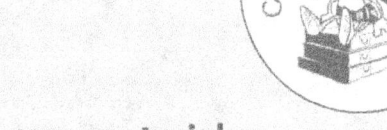

Time Needed

This FACTivity is meant to take a month to complete. The initial setup should take 1-2 class periods, and then it just takes a few minutes each day to monitor and record information.

Materials

- Five rain gauges or the materials to make rain gauges
- Paper for logbook or your science notebook

Rain gauge materials

- Five 2-liter bottles
- Tool to be able to cut top off plastic 2-liter bottles
- Duct tape
- Ruler
- Permanent marker
- Stones/ pebbles
- Water

The question you will answer in this FACTivity is: How much precipitation falls over a month's time at my school (or where I live)?

The method you will use to answer the question is:

1. Find five rain gauges. If you don't have rain gauges, you can easily make them. To make a rain gauge, follow these instructions. See the illustration on page 40.

2. Get a 2-liter plastic bottle and have an adult cut the top of the bottle off. Keep the top. Place duct tape around the areas that were cut so that sharp edges are covered.

3. Place pebbles or stones in the bottom of the bottle. These stones will help keep the bottle upright if it is windy outside.

4. On the bottom part of the bottle use a ruler to make a scale of horizontal lines. Start marking the lines from two inches above the bottom to two inches from the top. The lines should be separated by ½ inch.

5. Fill the bottom with water to the first line on your scale.

6. Next, place the cut off top upside down into the bottle. The upside down top creates a funnel. Now your rain gauge is ready.

7. Number your rain gauges from 1 to 5. Take two rain gauges and place them in flat areas away from buildings or trees. Take the other three rain

gauges and place them in flat areas underneath trees and near buildings.

8. Create a logbook so that you can keep track of the precipitation over an entire month. Make a separate page for each rain gauge and write the number of the gauge as well as a brief description of the area in which the rain gauge is located. Be sure to date each entry.

9. Each day, check the rain gauges to see whether water has evaporated from the rain gauge. If water has evaporated, then fill the gauge with water again to the first line. After it rains and you have taken your measurement, empty the rain gauge and fill to the first line. Doing this will help you make better measurements when it rains. Make a note in your logbook every time you have to fill up the water to the first line.

10. After a month, examine the data you collected. Create a graph for each rain gauge and the amount of precipitation.

As a class, discuss what you learned when you examined the data. Here are some questions to get you started.

- Were there really wet times and really dry times? Did you see the same thing with each of the rain gauges?

- How did different rain gauges compare?

- Did all the gauges get the same amount of precipitation? If not, why do you think they may be different?

- Did you have to fill certain rain gauges with water more often than others? If so, why do you think this is?

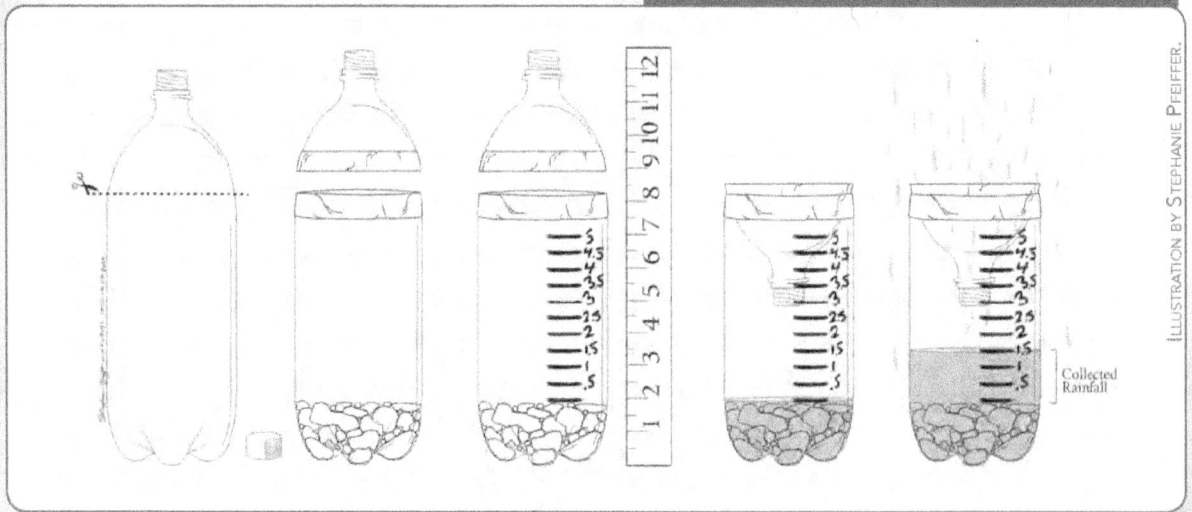

ILLUSTRATION BY STEPHANIE PFEIFFER.

Collected Rainfall

FACTivity Extension

You may want to continue this rain gauge project for a longer period of time. Additionally, you could compare your data to weather data that has been collected by the National Oceanic and Atmospheric Organization (NOAA). See the NOAA Web site for more information. http://water.weather.gov/precip/

Web Resources

Coweeta Long Term Ecological Research Web Site
http://coweeta.uga.edu/

Coweeta LTER Schoolyard Program
http://coweeta.uga.edu/lterschoolyard

U.S. Geological Survey (USGS) Water Cycle for Kids
http://ga.water.usgs.gov/edu/watercycle-kids.html

USGS Science in Your Watershed
http://water.usgs.gov/wsc/watersheds.html

Natural Inquirer **Ecosystem Services Edition**
http://www.naturalinquirer.org/Eco-i-26.html

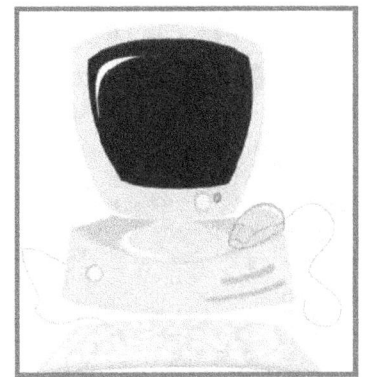

If you are a Project Learning Tree-trained educator, you may also use the following activity as an additional resource: "Field, Forest and Stream."

Fire and Water:

Predicting Future Wildfires in a Changing Climate

PHOTO COURTESY OF THE GILA NATIONAL FOREST.

What Kinds of Scientists Did this Research?

ecologist: This scientist studies the relationship of living things with their living and nonliving environment.

meteorologist: This scientist studies the atmosphere.

Thinking About Science

Predicting what might happen is a challenge. To plan for the future, a range of possibilities must be considered. Although we do not know for sure what the future will bring, we can plan for the future with many possibilities in mind.

Consider your own future. You might think, "If I get an A in English this year, I will be asked to join the school newspaper staff next year." Or, you might think, "If I get a D in English this year, I will not be allowed to join the soccer team next year." Along with these different possible futures, it is helpful to have some idea of how likely you are to earn either grade. Otherwise, you might have a difficult time planning for your future.

The scientists in this study wanted to predict the future likeliness of wildfires and where in the Southern United States these wildfires might occur. To do this, the scientists considered four possible futures. Each of these four possible futures was built on different ideas about what might happen in the future.

Each possible future was described by a model. A model is a simplified example of something. These four models were built from mathematical equations that described a possible future. Each model, for example, contained a different number **projecting** the human population in 2060. Each model also contained a different number projecting the average yearly air temperature in 2060. Using numbers to describe possible future conditions enables scientists to predict what might happen in the future.

Meet the Scientists

John Stanturf, ECOLOGIST:

My favorite science experience is getting to meet all kinds of people in many countries and seeing different kinds of forests.

Scott Goodrick, METEOROLOGIST:

My favorite science moment was when I first saw a time-lapse movie of clouds on TV when I was a kid. I watched a thunderstorm develop from a small puffy cloud to a majestic thunderhead over the course of a minute rather than an hour. Watching the cloud develop revealed some of the mysteries of these storms. Seeing things from a different perspective can open your eyes to new worlds.

Thinking About the Environment

Wildfires are a particular type of **wildland** fire. Some wildland fires are beneficial to a forest. This is because some kinds of forests need occasional fire to remain healthy (FIG. 1). Sometimes, wildland fires are purposefully set and managed to improve a forest's health. Beneficial fires burn at low temperatures and their flames stay close to the ground. These fires help to clean out brush and wood lying on the ground, but do not damage large trees. When fires are purposefully set, they are managed so that they can be easily put out. These kind of fires are called prescribed fires (FIG. 2).

Wildfires are a different kind of wildland fire. Wildfires may be **ignited** naturally, such as by lightning. They may also be ignited by careless human acts. Wildfires burn at high temperatures. Their flames reach high into **tree crowns** (FIG. 3). Wildfires are difficult to control and **extinguish**, and they may cause a lot of environmental and **economic** damage.

FIGURE 1. A LONGLEAF PINE FOREST NEEDS OCCASIONAL FIRE TO REMAIN HEALTHY. PHOTO BY RICKY LAYSON AND COURTESY OF HTTP://WWW.BUGWOOD.ORG.

FIGURE 2. A PRESCRIBED FIRE IS PURPOSEFULLY SET BY FORESTERS TO MANAGE THE FOREST. PHOTO BY DAVID CAPPAERT AND COURTESY OF HTTP://WWW.BUGWOOD.ORG.

FIGURE 3. WILDFIRES ARE LARGE WILDLAND FIRES WHOSE FLAMES REACH HIGH INTO TREE CROWNS. PHOTO COURTESY OF THE GEORGIA FORESTRY COMMISSION ARCHIVE AND HTTP://WWW.BUGWOOD.ORG

Introduction

Wildfires often occur during times of **drought**. When rainfall is low, trees, wood lying on the ground, and **leaf litter** are drier, and therefore are more likely to burn (FIG. 4). Wildfires are more likely when droughts occur and during periods of high temperatures.

Successfully predicting where and when wildfires might occur is important. This prediction is important because of possible environmental and economic damage. As the climate warms, the possibility of wildfires might increase. The scientists in this study wanted to predict where and in what seasons wildfires might occur.

The scientists were particularly interested in the Southern United States (FIG. 5). Wildfires across the Southern United States burn fewer hectares than are burned in the Western United States (FIG. 6). These southern fires, however, destroy many more homes and buildings than western wildfires. The scientists wanted to look 50 years into the future to the year 2060.

FIGURE 4. WOOD LYING ON THE FOREST FLOOR, ALONG WITH LEAF LITTER, PROVIDES FUEL FOR WILDFIRES. PHOTO BY BABS MCDONALD.

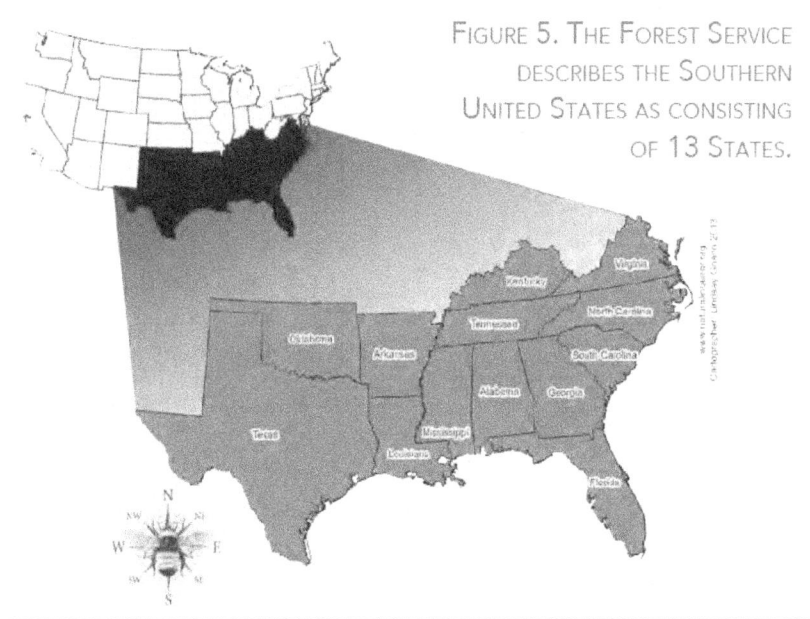

FIGURE 5. THE FOREST SERVICE DESCRIBES THE SOUTHERN UNITED STATES AS CONSISTING OF 13 STATES.

Number Crunch

▶ How old will you be in 2060?

How Big Is a Hectare?

Figure 6. A hectare is a little smaller than a soccer field. One hectare is equal to 2.47 acres.

Reflection Section
Reflection Section

⇨ Why do you think southern wildfires burn more homes and buildings than western wildfires?

⇨ In what ways could wildfires affect you in 2060?

⇨ How might the successful prediction of wildfires be helpful to communities?

Methods

If the climate were not changing, scientists might predict that there would be no change in the occurrence of wildfires. Because the climate is changing, scientists believe that the occurrence of wildfires will change. An aspect of climate change of particular importance to wildfire prediction is rising temperatures. As average temperatures rise, the possibility of drought rises as well.

To predict potential wildfires, the scientists considered four possible futures (FIG. 7). These futures were based on different climate change models. A climate change model is a mathematical equation that makes different **assumptions** about weather and other conditions over time.

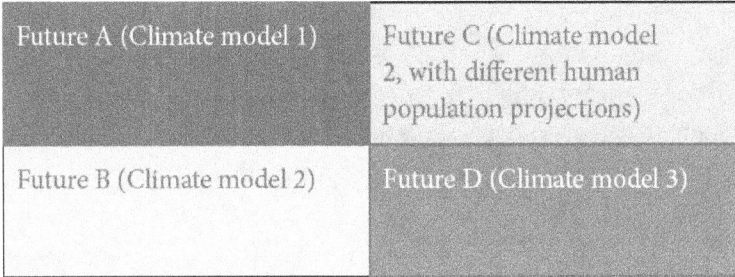

Future A (Climate model 1)	Future C (Climate model 2, with different human population projections)
Future B (Climate model 2)	Future D (Climate model 3)

FIGURE 7. THE FOUR POSSIBLE FUTURES WERE LABELED A, B, C, AND D. EACH OF THESE FUTURES WAS BASED ON A CLIMATE CHANGE MODEL. EACH MODEL MAKES DIFFERENT ASSUMPTIONS ABOUT THE FUTURE. EACH CLIMATE CHANGE MODEL, FOR EXAMPLE, **ASSUMES** THAT THE TEMPERATURE WILL RISE BY A DIFFERENT NUMBER OF DEGREES. EACH ASSUMES DIFFERENT PATTERNS OF RAINFALL. BECAUSE SCIENTISTS DO NOT KNOW FOR SURE WHAT WILL HAPPEN IN THE FUTURE, THEY CONSIDER DIFFERENT POSSIBLE FUTURES.

The scientists then measured the potential for wildfire in each of these possible futures. This measurement took two things into account. These two things are potential evapotranspiration (ē **vap** ō tran spïr **ā** shən) and how much **precipitation** is predicted to fall (FIG. 8).

The scientists calculated potential evapotranspiration based on the predicted weather variables in each of the four models. The scientists then subtracted predicted precipitation from potential evapotranspiration for each model.

What Is the Difference Between Weather and Climate?

The difference between weather and climate is a measure of time. Weather is the conditions in the atmosphere over a short amount of time. Weather includes daily temperatures, relative humidity, and wind speed, for example. Climate is a long-term average of weather measurements. Climate change is changes in the long-term average of weather measurements.

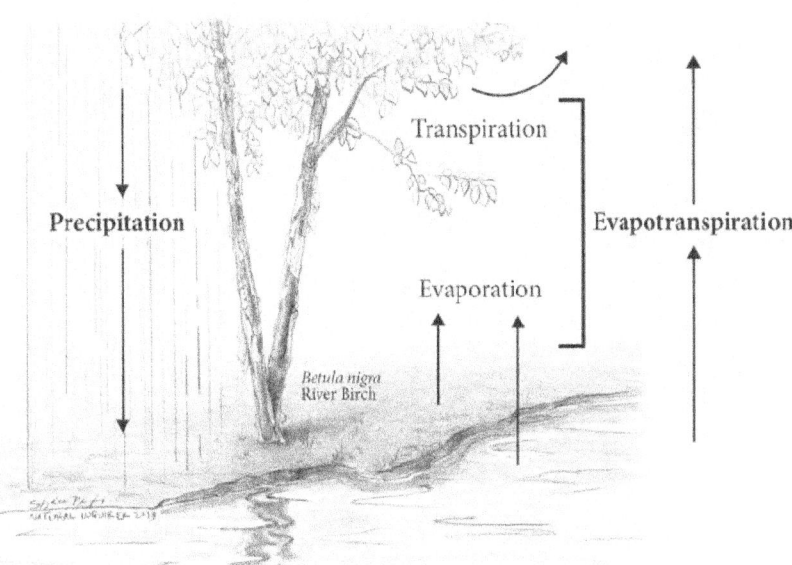

FIGURE 8. POTENTIAL EVAPOTRANSPIRATION IS A MEASURE OF HOW MUCH WATER CAN MOVE FROM THE SURFACE OF EARTH TO THE ATMOSPHERE. PRECIPITATION IS A MEASURE OF HOW MUCH WATER MOVES FROM THE ATMOSPHERE TO EARTH. ILLUSTRATION BY STEPHANIE PFEIFFER.

What Is Potential Evapotranspiration?

Potential evapotranspiration is a measurement used by scientists to determine how much evaporation would occur from our planet's surface if enough water was available. Potential evapotranspiration is affected by temperature, wind, and other weather **variables**. It is not affected, however, by the amount of water available because adequate water supply is assumed.

Reflection Section

Reflection Section

 Why did the scientists consider four possible futures instead of just one?

 What is the relationship between precipitation and wildfire?

In drier areas, potential evapotranspiration is higher than precipitation (FIG. 9). Drier areas may be more likely to experience wildfires. Using this process, the scientists identified areas in the Southern United States that may be more likely to have wildfires. They used this process for each of the four possible futures in the year 2060.

FIGURE 9. WHEN POTENTIAL EVAPOTRANSPIRATION IS GREATER THAN PRECIPITATION, AN AREA EXPERIENCES DROUGHT (A). WHEN POTENTIAL EVAPOTRANSPIRATION IS LESS THAN PRECIPITATION, AN AREA EXPERIENCES WET CONDITIONS (B). YOU WILL NOTICE IN PHOTO B THAT THERE IS A LIGHTER AREA AT THE FRONT OF THE PHOTO. THIS LIGHTER COLORED AREA IS WATER. PHOTOS COURTESY OF TOM MILLER, UNIVERSITY OF KENTUCKY, AND HTTP://WWW.BUGWOOD.ORG (A), AND DAREN MUELLER, IOWA STATE UNIVERSITY, AND HTTP://WWW.BUGWOOD.ORG (B).

Findings

All four possible futures showed similar wildfire potential in 2010 (FIG. 10A). Areas in the western part of the Southern United States had a higher potential for wildfire because of drier conditions and higher temperatures.

Prescribed fire is used frequently in the South to reduce the amount of fuel on the ground. As the wildfire season gets longer in the future, the need for fuel reduction will be greater. Unfortunately, drier conditions will also make using prescribed fire more dangerous. Some of the greater dangers of prescribed fire in drier conditions include the following:

- More chance of fire escaping

- More damage to natural and human-built resources

- More smoke-related air pollution, causing health problems

- More smoke in the air, creating dangerous driving conditions

Instead of using prescribed fire, managers may need to use other procedures to reduce ground-level fuels. Other procedures include cutting or chopping and removing ground-level plants or using chemicals to kill the plants. Unfortunately, these other methods usually cost more than prescribed fire, and these methods provide fewer environmental benefits than prescribed fire.

If the chance for wildfire increases into the future, more fires will contribute even more to climate change. When forests are green and growing, they hold carbon on Earth. When trees and other plants are burned by wildfire or prescribed fire, the carbon contained in the trees is released into the atmosphere.

To better understand how conditions might change in the future, the scientists compared the map of wildfire potential in 2060 (FIG. 10B) with the map of areas experiencing wildfires in 2010 (FIG. 10A, PAGE 50).

The scientists found that, in 2060, the driest areas were not always the areas with wildfires. Dry areas may have little vegetation and therefore no fuel to burn in a wildfire. Areas predicted to have the greatest number of burned hectares were areas with the most precipitation. Many hectares burn in these areas because high precipitation causes forest growth. Many trees provide a lot of fuel for wildfires.

In 2060, all four possible futures predicted drier conditions than in 2010. Future A showed the most extreme dry conditions. All of the areas experiencing wildfires in 2010 are predicted to become drier in 2060 with a higher potential for wildfire.

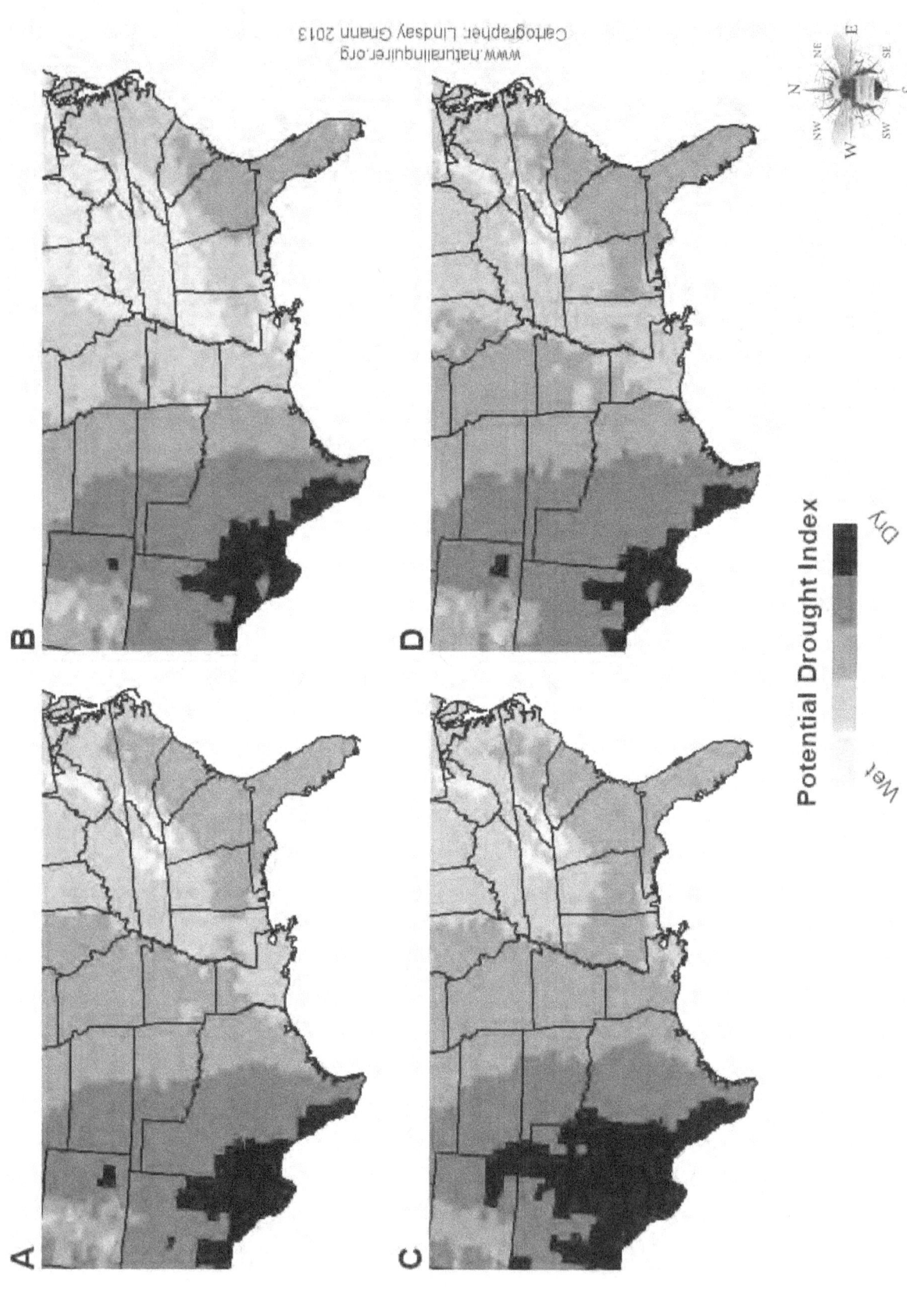

Potential Drought Index

Wet ... Dry

Cartographer: Lindsay Gnann 2013
www.naturalinquirer.org

FIGURE 10A. WILDFIRE POTENTIAL AS A FUNCTION OF POTENTIAL DROUGHT IN THE SOUTHERN UNITED STATES IN 2010 FOR FOUR POSSIBLE FUTURES.

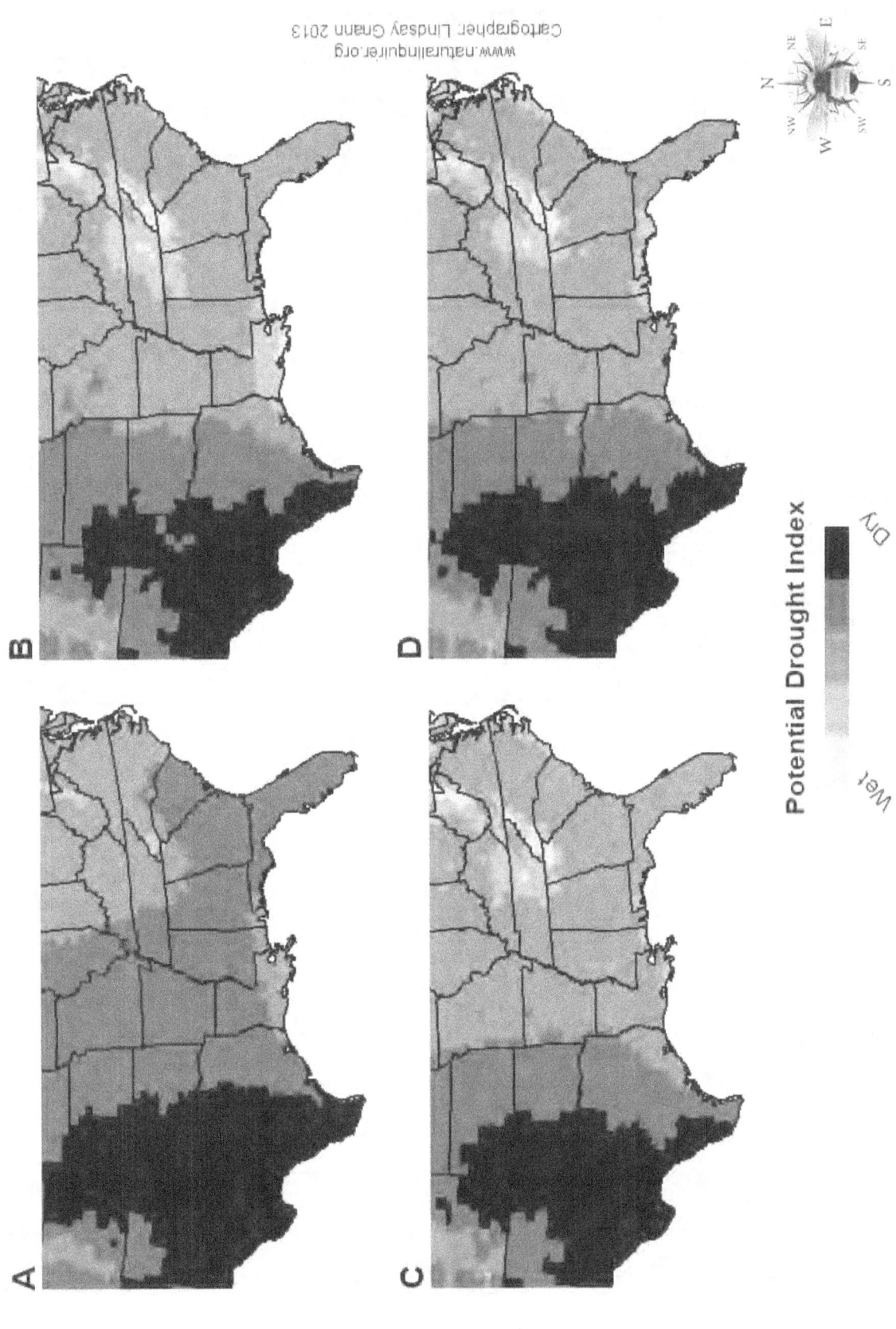

www.naturalinquirer.org
Cartographer: Lindsay Gnann 2013

Potential Drought Index

Wet — Dry

Figure 10b. Wildfire potential as a function of potential drought in the Southern United States in 2060 for four possible futures.

Reflection Section

Reflection Section

➡ If areas currently experiencing wildfires become drier in the future, what will happen to the wildfire potential?

➡ Look at figure 10b. What landform is predicted to be the South's wettest area in 2060? If you do not know, look at the **topographic** map below. What is it about this landform that creates a wetter area?

Discussion

The scientists concluded that wildfire risk will increase slightly over the next 50 years. The scientists also predicted that rising temperatures will increase the chance of wildfires occurring in the spring and fall. If this happens, the risk for wildfires will be higher in the spring, summer, and fall of each year.

The population of the Southern United States is predicted to rise. More urban development in and near forests is expected. A rising population and more development will mean more people living in and near forests. The scientists caution that more people could mean more wildfires because some careless actions can cause wildfires, and more people will be living near and in forests.

Reflection Section

 According to this research, how is a changing climate affecting the future potential for wildfire in the Southern United States?

 The scientists noted that more people living in the Southern United States may mean two things: more wildfires being ignited by careless people and more homes and buildings near and in forests. What is one thing that could be done to reduce the number of potential wildfires?

Adapted from Stanturf, J.A.; Goodrick, S.L.[In press]. Fire. In: Wear, David N.; Greis, John G., eds. The Southern Forest Futures Project: Technical Report. Gen. Tech. Rep. SRS-178. Asheville, NC: U.S. Department of Agriculture Forest Service, Southern Research Station. http://www.srs fs.usda.gov/futures/reports/draft/pdf/technicalreport.pdf

Glossary

assume (ə **süm**): To take information as granted or true.

assumption (ə **səm(p)** shən): A fact or statement taken for granted.

drought (**draut**): A period of dry weather with little or no rain.

economic (e kə **nä** mik): Of, relating to, or based on the production, distribution, and consumption of goods and services.

evident (**ev** ə dent): Clear to the sight or the mind.

extinguish (ik **stiŋ** (g)wish): To bring to an end.

ignite (ig **nīt**): To cause to burn.

leaf litter (**lēf li** tər): The top layer of dead and decaying leaves, small sticks, and twigs that lay on the forest floor.

precipitation (pri **si** pə **tā** shən): Rain, hail, snow, mist, or sleet.

project (prə **jekt**): To plan, figure, or estimate for the future.

topographic (tō pə **gra** fik): Of, related to, or concerned with the physical features that make up the topography (tə **pä** grə fē) of an area, such as mountains, valleys, plains, and bodies of water.

tree crown (**trē kraun**): The upper green section of a tree with leaves or needles.

variable (**ver** ē ə bəl): Something that is able or apt to vary.

wildland (**wīld land**): Forested or other natural environment that does not contain buildings or other human construction.

Accented syllables are in **bold**. Marks and definitions are from http://www.merriam-webster.com.

FACTivity

Common Core Connection

Time Needed
1 class period, more time may be needed for independent research

Materials

- Blank paper or science notebook

- Pencil

- Poster board

- Felt markers (various colors)

- Access to media center or the Internet

The question you will answer in this FACTivity is: How would I use technology to communicate wildland fire safety in the year 2050?

Background

The Forest Service is an agency of the U.S. Department of Agriculture. The Forest Service has three main branches. Research and Development is one of the branches. The research in this article was done by scientists working in the Research and Development branch of the Forest Service. Another Forest Service branch is called State and Private Forestry. Educators working in this branch communicate important information to students and adults. Often, these educators develop educational materials based on the work of Forest Service scientists.

In this FACTivity, you will time-travel to the year 2050. The scientists who conducted this research predicted certain things might happen by the year 2060. By the year 2050, most of the predicted changes will likely be **evident**. If you need to review the scientists' predictions, reread the "Findings" and "Discussion" sections on pages 49-53.

Methods

It is the year 2050. You are a wildland fire safety educator with the Forest Service. You have decided to develop a wildfire safety poster and distribute it to students across the United States.

First, review the scientists' wildfire and climate predictions in this article. You should do additional research in the media center or on the Internet. Good Web sites to visit are http://www.smokeybear.com/wildfires.asp and http://www.firewise.org/information.aspx. Using felt markers and poster board, create an educational poster about wildfires and wildfire safety. You may also use magazine photos and other resources to create a collage.

Back in the second decade of the 21st century, almost 40 years ago, technology such as smartphones and tablets were changing the way people communicated. Now, in the year 2050, technology has advanced even more. Use your imagination to develop a plan using this advanced technology to distribute your poster to students across the United States.

The first step will be to organize into small groups of 3 to 5 students. Brainstorm for 5 minutes to generate ideas for how and what technology will be used in 2050. When you brainstorm, do not criticize others and let your creative juices flow! You should assign one group member to record your group's ideas. The remainder of the FACTivity may be done individually or in your small group.

Use the graphic organizer in this FACTivity to help you develop your plan. Then, write out your plan using complete sentences, proper grammar, and proper punctuation. If you have time, make oral presentations to the class, describing how technology is helping you to educate others about wildfire safety.

Then, draw your poster using the blank paper and markers. Present your plan and poster to your class. Post the posters in your school. What new technology did you develop? Hold a class discussion about how technology might aid education in the future. Note: You may also send a photo of your poster to jessica@naturalinquirer.org. Some of these posters may be chosen for display on our Web site.

Web Resources

Smokey Bear and Wildfire Information
http://www.smokeybear.com/wildfires.asp

Firewise Communities Information
http://www.firewise.org/information.aspx

Fire Adapted Communities
http://www.fireadapted.org

If you are a trained Project Learning Tree-educator, you may use *Living with Fire* as an additional resource.

Graphic Organizer for Wildfire Safety Education Plan, 2050

What is the wildfire situation in 2050? (For example, are wildfires frequent? Is the average temperature warmer than it was in the second decade of the century so that wildfires are more likely? Are wildfires less likely? Why?)
What is the specific topic of your poster? Develop this topic from your research in the media center or on the Internet.
What are the two main messages of your poster?
What grade level(s) will you reach with your poster?
Your poster will be digitized or otherwise turned into an electronic file. What new technology will you use to share the digital file? Identify at least one technology that you will use in 2050.

Wildfire Safety Education Plan

This Plan Was Developed By:

Poster Title

Specific Poster Topic

Primary Poster Messages

Primary Audience (Grade Level, Type of School)

Digitized Filename

Describe How Your Electronic Poster File Will Be Distributed

Wide Open Spaces:

Climate Change Impacts in Rural Areas of the United States

PHOTO BY BABS MCDONALD

What Kinds of Scientists Did This Research?

economist: This scientist studies economics. Economics is a social science that addresses the production, distribution, and use of goods and services.

policy analyst: This scientist compares different policies to determine which **policy** will best help achieve an identified set of goals.

Thinking About Science

When scientists begin their research, they read as much as possible of what has already been written on the topic. This process is important because it allows the scientists to make sure they are up-to-date on all the newest research. In some cases, the topic the scientists are interested in has so much information that reading, understanding, and tying all the information together becomes a research project in itself. In this study, scientists read and compiled information and research on climate and rural areas. The scientists wanted to examine how climate change may affect rural areas and the people that live there.

Thinking About the Environment

Every living thing has basic things it needs to survive. Animals need air, water, food, and shelter. Plants need air, water, nutrients, and light. To do well and prosper, however, living things need a good habitat in which to live. A good habitat means that there is food and water available and that the climate is suitable for the living thing. As the climate changes, some living things may move to different habitats if they can. In this study, the scientists examined a particular group of living things and what might happen if their environment changes. The scientists looked at how rural areas in the United States and people living in rural areas may be affected by climate change.

Meet the Scientist

Pankaj Lal, ENVIRONMENT AND FOREST RESOURCE ECONOMIST:

My favorite science experience is using the principles of **economics** to solve environmental problems. These problems include **deforestation,** other natural resource **depletion**, climate change, and pollution control. I believe that the economy and environment can go together. I love working on policy options that can be used to solve environmental problems.

Introduction

The United States is made up of both rural and urban areas. Rural areas are areas with fewer people and more land (FIG. 1). Urban areas are areas with a high population density (FIGS. 2A AND 2B). For this research, the scientists identified 2,050 counties in the United States that were rural and 1,090 counties that were urban (FIG. 3). Rural areas make up about 17 percent of the population in the United States but cover 80 percent of the land area.

FIGURE 1. RURAL AREA IN GEORGIA. PHOTO BY BABS McDONALD.

FIGURE 2A. URBAN AREA IN HELSINKI, FINLAND. PHOTO BY BABS McDONALD.

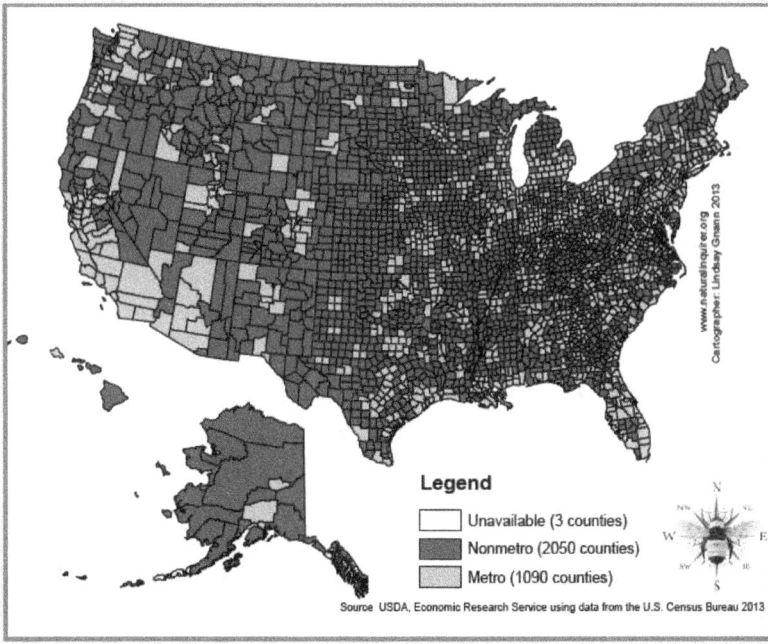

FIGURE 2B. URBAN AREA IN WASHINGTON, D.C.
PHOTO BY BABS MCDONALD.

Legend

Unavailable (3 counties)
Nonmetro (2050 counties)
Metro (1090 counties)

Source USDA, Economic Research Service using data from the U.S. Census Bureau 2013

FIGURE 3. THE RURAL COUNTIES ARE IN DARK GRAY AND CALLED NONMETRO. METRO INDICATES A MORE URBAN AREA. FIND WHERE YOU LIVE ON THE MAP. ARE YOU IN AN URBAN AREA OR A RURAL AREA?

What is the Pareto (pə rā tō) Principle?

Have you ever heard of the 80-20 rule? This rule is also called the Pareto Principle. The Pareto Principle was coined in 1941 by Joseph Juran. He named the principle after an Italian named Vilfredo Pareto. In 1906, Pareto observed that 80 percent of Italy's land was owned by 20 percent of the population. Pareto also observed that 20 percent of the pea pods in his garden contained 80 percent of the peas. The rule has come to describe the observation that 80 percent of an effect comes from 20 percent of the cause.

In this study, a little less than 20 percent of the United States population was identified as living on 80 percent of the country's land area. Think about your classroom. About 80 percent of the time, do the same 20 percent of students raise their hand? Be on the lookout for examples of the Pareto Principle!

Rural counties tend to be poorer than urban counties. Rural counties also have higher unemployment, lower educational **attainment**, fewer highly skilled jobs, and greater dependency on government funds. Because of the **socioeconomic** challenges rural areas face, these areas may be vulnerable to climate change in some ways while not as vulnerable in other ways. When something is vulnerable, it is open to attack or damage. For example, rural areas are expected to experience more negative impacts from the change in agriculture due to climate change than urban areas experience. However, rural areas may not experience as many extreme heat events as urban areas. The scientists in this study were interested in studying how climate change may impact rural areas in the United States.

Reflection Section
Reflection Section

 What were the scientists interested in learning from this research?

 Do you live in an urban or rural area? How do you know?

Methods

The scientists collected journal articles, government reports, and other publications about climate change. The scientists read all of the information and organized it into three areas. The three areas were human health, **indigenous** communities, and economic impacts. Much of the literature did not specifically address social and economic effects of climate change, so the scientists made **inferences** about these effects.

The inferences were based on general climate models (GCMs). GCMs are computer models that allow people to create long-term weather forecasts and predict future changes in climate. These models use mathematical equations to **simulate** the interactions of things like water, atmosphere, land surfaces, and ice. These equations are then run through computers and interpreted by scientists.

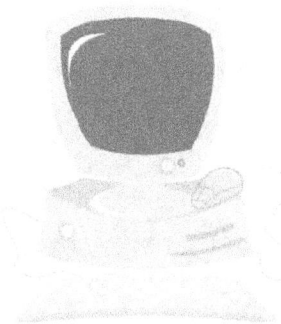

Reflection Section

Reflection Section

⇨ Think of a time when you have made a model. (For example, you may have made a model of a cell, the solar system, a mathematical model, or a model of a historical event.) How did creating this model help you better understand what you were learning?

⇨ The scientists in this research used evidence and reasoning to draw inferences about how climate change may affect rural areas and the people living there. An inference is a conclusion reached based on evidence and reasoning. Think of a time when you used evidence and reasoning to infer a particular conclusion. Write two sentences describing when and why you used inference. Do you think this is a good way to draw conclusions? Why or why not?

PHOTO BY BABS MCDONALD

What Is the Heat Island Effect?

The heat island effect refers to the fact that concrete and asphalt in cities absorb and hold heat. The tall buildings in cities prevent heat from **dissipating**. Air flow is also reduced. All of these elements combine to create an area of greater heat (FIG. 5). According to the U.S. Environmental Protection Agency, areas that experience the heat island effect can have a mean annual temperature 1.8-5.4 °F higher than surrounding rural areas. For additional information, visit http://www.epa.gov/hiri/.

Findings

The scientists made a variety of inferences and determinations based on the climate change literature they read. Below you will read about some of the inferences they made about rural areas in each of the following areas: impacts on human health, impacts on indigenous populations, and economic impacts.

Impacts on Human Health

The scientists looked at direct and indirect impacts when they studied human health impacts in rural areas. The scientists found that direct impacts resulted from increased exposure to temperature and extreme weather. The scientists found that rural areas may be less vulnerable to extreme heat events than cities due to the heat island effect. Additionally, rural areas typically have more vegetation. The increased vegetation provides more shade and cooling from evaporation (FIGS. 4A AND 4B).

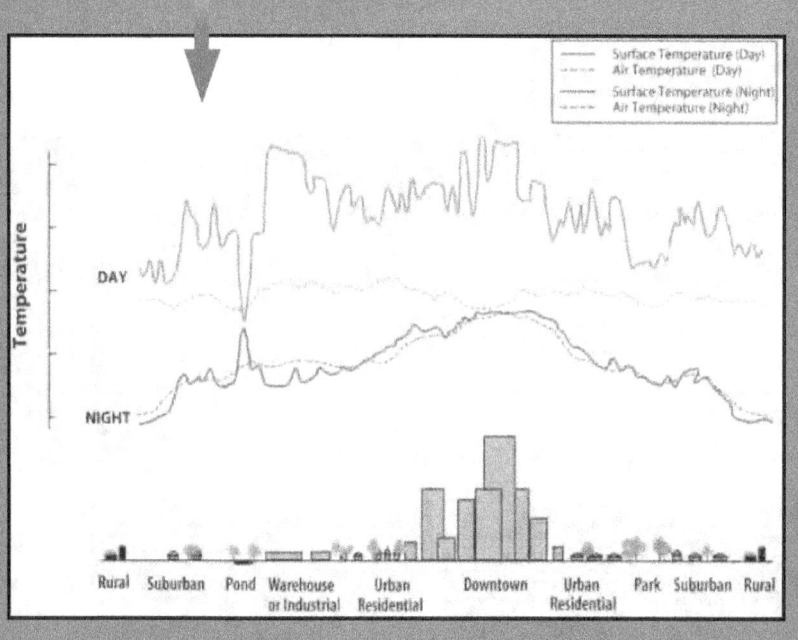

FIGURE 5. LOOK AT THE GRAPH. NOTICE THE DIFFERENCE BETWEEN THE DAYTIME AND NIGHTTIME SURFACE TEMPERATURE IN URBAN VERSUS RURAL AREAS. WHAT ELSE DO YOU NOTICE IN THIS GRAPH? GRAPH COURTESY OF THE U.S. ENVIRONMENTAL PROTECTION AGENCY.

FIGURE 4A.
RURAL AREA WITH
VEGETATION IN
ALASKA.
PHOTO BY BABS MCDONALD.

FIGURE 4B.
RURAL AREA WITH
VEGETATION IN
NORTH CAROLINA.
PHOTO BY BABS MCDONALD.

The scientists also found that indirect impacts from disease and infection could potentially have a negative impact on rural communities. Heavy downpours, for example, could lead to an increase in **sediment** runoff into waterways. This increase in sediment in the waterways could lead to an increase in waterborne diseases.

Impacts on Indigenous Communities

Many indigenous communities are located in rural areas. The scientists found that communities such as Native American communities and Native Alaskan communities may experience negative impacts from climate change. For example, it is estimated that climate change may increase flooding and erosion by 86 percent in Native Alaskan communities (FIG. 6).

FIGURE 6. ALASKA HAS BEAUTIFUL LANDSCAPES. NOTICE THE ARCTIC GROUND SQUIRREL IN THE PHOTO. NATIVE ALASKANS AND OTHERS LIVING IN ALASKA MAY SEE THIS LANDSCAPE CHANGE AS A RESULT OF A CHANGING CLIMATE. PHOTO BY TIM RAINS, NATIONAL PARK SERVICE.

Native American communities and other indigenous communities are not as flexible in terms of moving to different areas. In the case of Native Americans, some of these people live on land that is specially protected for them (FIG. 7). Therefore, if the climate changes and creates problems in the area that they live, they may not be as likely to change location as some other people. Additionally, access to traditional food sources and ways of collecting and sharing food may be impacted.

Economic Impacts

The scientists examined six different areas in the category of economic impacts. The scientists examined **agriculture**, recreation and tourism, **forestry**, water, **fisheries**, and energy. Below are examples from the two areas of agriculture and forestry.

Agriculture takes place largely in rural areas because of the amount of land required for agricultural activities. The impact of climate change on agricultural activities, therefore, directly affects rural areas. Some crop plants, for example, may not

FIGURE 7. QUALLA BOUNDARY OF THE CHEROKEE INDIAN RESERVATION.
PHOTO COURTESY OF RICHARD WEISSER AND HTTP://WWW.SMOKYPHOTOS.COM.

be able to grow in areas that they traditionally grew in due to increases in the average temperature. The change in crop location may benefit where crops are able to grow and may benefit some rural areas while it may **devastate** other rural areas. Additionally, a warming climate may cause crops to develop and bloom too early which may expose these plants to late season frosts. Another example can be found in the dairy industry. The dairy industry can be affected by climate change because dairy cows' productivity decreases when the temperature goes above 77 °F.

Another area of possible economic impact for rural areas is forestry. Depending on how the temperature changes due to climate change, scientists have made projections about what types of trees will grow in different areas (FIG. 8). If forests in the South and Northeast shift to oak and hickory trees instead of **softwoods** like pine trees, then the wood and **pulp** industry may experience large losses. These losses would impact rural communities because many people in these rural areas make their living from working in the wood and pulp industry.

Number Crunch

Dairy cows' productivity decreases when temperatures go above 77 °F. What is that temperature in °C? The equation you should use is °C = (°F-32) x 5/9.

FIGURE 8. LOOK AT EACH OF THE STATES. COMPARE THE RECENT PAST TO THE PROJECTED FUTURE. WHAT DO YOU NOTICE ABOUT HOW THE TREE SPECIES WILL CHANGE?

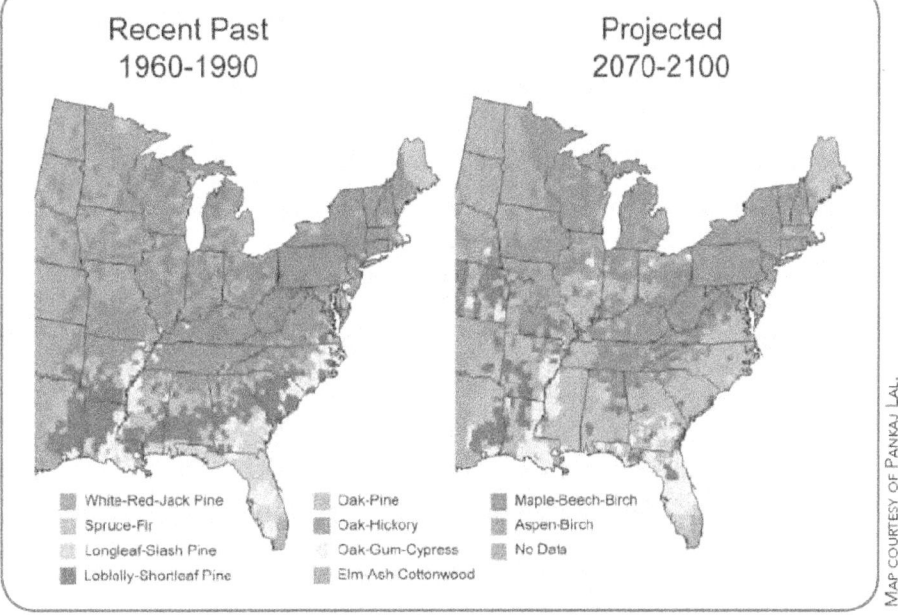

MAP COURTESY OF PANKAJ LAL.

Reflection Section
Reflection Section

 Look at figure 8. According to this map, how would the areas of loblolly-shortleaf pine change if the climate changes as the scientists have projected? How do you think these changes would affect these areas?

 Reread the sidebar on the heat island effect. Name one way you think cities could help reduce this effect. Why do you think your idea will help?

Discussion

The potential impacts of climate change on rural areas include increased risks to human health, changes to agriculture and forestry, and increased demand on water resources. Other potential impacts include those from increased stress on fisheries, changes to tourism and recreation, negative effects on indigenous communities, and other **adverse** impacts related to extreme weather events.

The scientists recommend doing additional research that focuses on rural areas' ability to adapt to climate change. Researchers need to look at the costs of adapting to climate change. They also should explore what problems may arise when rural communities adapt to this change, and the consequences of climate change for rural communities. This type of research would allow rural communities to prepare for a changing climate and may help reduce negative impacts from climate change.

The scientists also recommend examining alternative energy sources as a way to help rural areas. Solar energy and wind energy, for example, may help reduce the negative impacts of climate change on rural areas. The scientists warn, however, that the focus on alternative energy should take into account the predictions for climate change.

The scientists recommend that some policies should be developed to help rural areas adapt to a changing climate. With these policies in place, rural areas will be better prepared for the potential impacts of climate change and may be able to more quickly adapt and respond to changes.

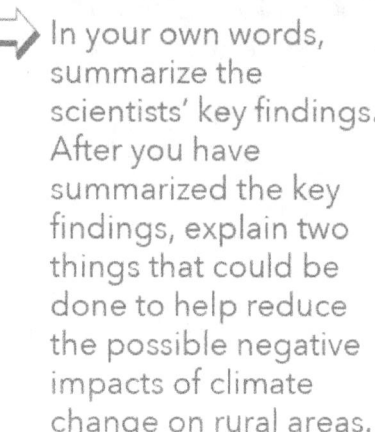

Reflection Section

⇨ In your own words, summarize the scientists' key findings. After you have summarized the key findings, explain two things that could be done to help reduce the possible negative impacts of climate change on rural areas.

⇨ Think about a time when you had to adapt to a change. For example, maybe you changed schools or moved to a different town. How did planning help you adapt to this change? Why do you think the scientists recommend planning for the impacts of climate change on rural areas?

Extreme Weather Events in the News

In October and November 2012, Hurricane Sandy moved up the Eastern United States coastline. In November 2013, Typhoon Haiyan moved across the Philippines in the Western Pacific Ocean and into Vietnam. Some people wondered if these two extreme weather events, which caused damage to human communities and to the environment, were related to climate change. On the Internet or in your school's media center, conduct research on these and other recent extreme weather events. Share your findings with your classmates. Hold a class discussion about extreme weather events and climate change. Do you think they are related? Why or why not?

Glossary

adverse (ad **vərs**): Results in negative effects.

agriculture (**a** gri **kəl** chər): The science or practice of preparing the soil, producing crops, and raising livestock.

attainment (ə **tān** mənt): To have possession of.

deforestation (dē **for** ə **stā** shən): The action or process of clearing of forests. Deforestation happens when a forest is destroyed and the area previously occupied by the trees is used for other purposes.

depletion (de **plē** shən): The state of having most or all of something being used.

devastate (**de** və stāt): To ruin or destroy.

dissipate (**di** sə pāt): To break up and scatter or vanish.

economics (**e** kə **nä** miks): The study of the way that goods, services, and wealth are produced, distributed, and used.

fisheries (**fi** shə rēz): Places for catching fish or other sea animals.

forestry (**for** ə strē): The science and management of growing trees and timber.

indigenous (in **di** jə nəs): Produced, growing, living, or occurring naturally in a particular region or environment.

inference (**in** f(ə-) rən(t)s): Conclusion or opinion that is formed because of known facts or evidence.

policy (**pä** lə sē): Overall plan with rules that must be followed, generally made by a government.

pulp (**pəlp**): A material prepared by chemical or mechanical means from various materials (such as wood) for use in making paper products.

sediment (**se** də mənt): Material deposited by water, wind, or glaciers.

simulate (**sim** yə lāt): To create the appearance or effect of something for purposes of evaluation.

socioeconomic (**sō** sē ō e kə **nä** mik): Of, relating to, or involving a combination of social and economic factors.

softwood (**soft** wüd): Coniferous tree (such as fir or pine).

Accented syllables are in **bold**. Marks and definitions are from http://www.merriam-webster.com.

Web Resources

PBS Harriman Expedition Retraced- Alaska Native Communities
http://www.pbs.org/harriman/1899/native.html

U.S. Environmental Protection Agency (EPA) Heat Island Effect
http://www.epa.gov/hiri/

National Aeronautics and Space Agency (NASA) Climate Kids
http://climatekids.nasa.gov/

U.S. Environmental Protection Agency Climate Change Kids Site
http://www.kidsnewsroom.org/climatechange/

If you are a Project Learning Tree-trained educator, you may also use the following activities as an added resource: "Our Changing World" or "The Global Climate."

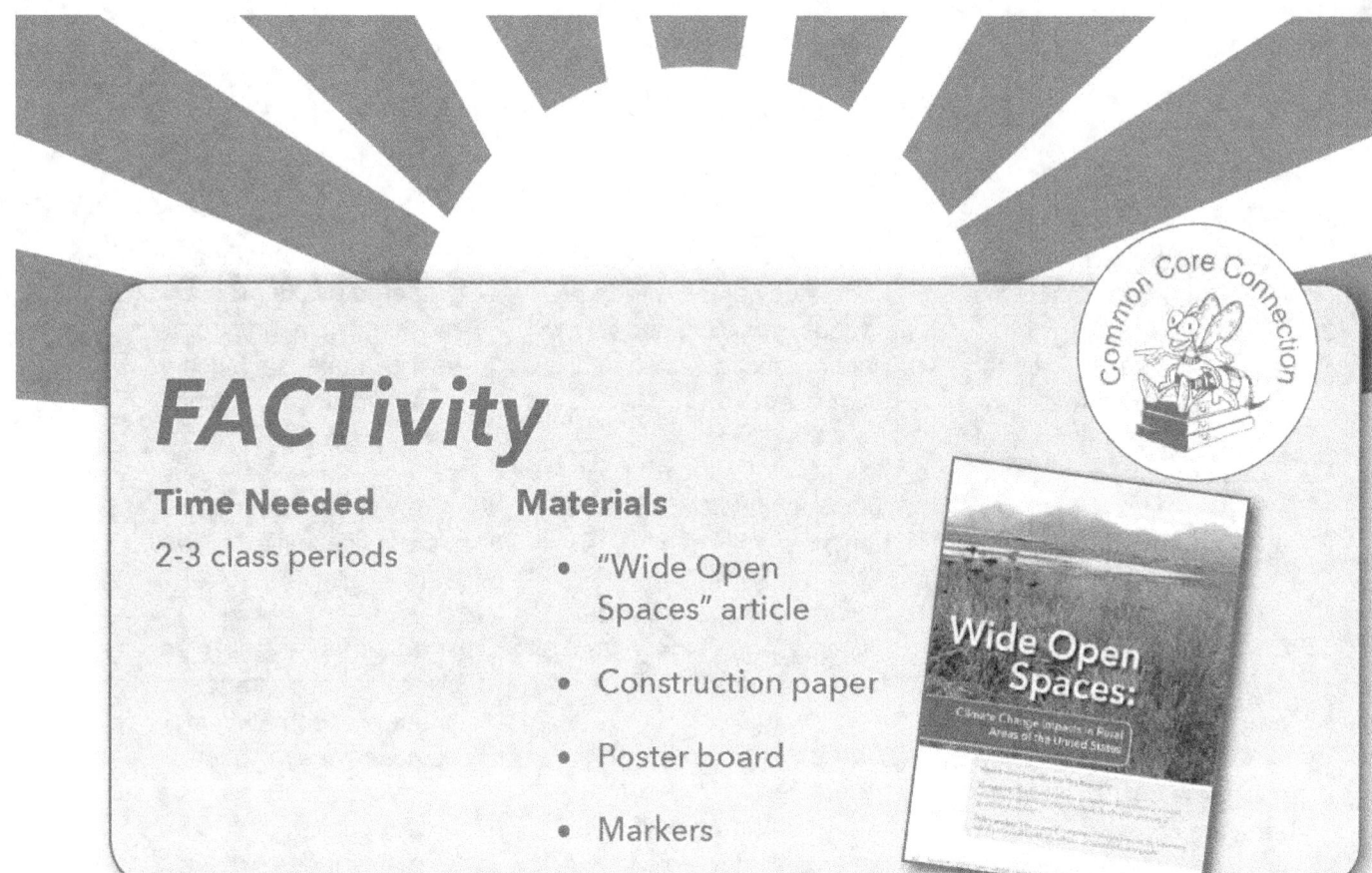

FACTivity

Time Needed

2-3 class periods

Materials

- "Wide Open Spaces" article
- Construction paper
- Poster board
- Markers

Common Core Connection

Wide Open Spaces: Climate Change Impacts in Rural Areas of the United States

The question you will answer in this FACTivity is:
How do I effectively explain the possible effects of climate change to people that live in rural areas?

To create awareness and an educated public, officials often create informational brochures and hold public meetings to inform people about different topics. For this FACTivity, you can choose to either create an informational brochure or create a presentation to inform people in rural areas about the possible impacts of climate change.

The method you will use to answer this question is:

1) You will work in small groups. In your small groups, decide if you would like to create an informational brochure or create a presentation. You will create your presentation on poster board. You will create your brochure using construction paper.

2) Either product that you choose to work on must include the following components:

   a. A brief introduction to the topic of climate change.

b. A brief overview of rural areas.

c. A discussion of at least two out of the three areas of impact that are covered in the article.

d. A discussion about things that could be done to help reduce the negative effects of climate change. You should provide at least 2 examples.

e. A graph.

f. Two pictures.

g. A map.

3) After you have completed your product, your teacher may have you present it to the class or share it with another group in your class.

4) As a whole class, discuss why it is important to provide information to the general public about different topics. Also discuss what some of the challenges may be to providing this type of information.

A possible extension is to incorporate technology into this project, if you have access to computers and the Internet. If this is a possibility, then you may want to create a digital presentation, digital brochure, or create an informational Web page.

FACTivity Extension

If you live in a rural area, write a letter to community officials and tell them what you have learned and share your presentation or informational brochure with them. Use proper form in your letter, as well as proper sentence structure, spelling, and punctuation. If you live in an urban area, look around you and see if you think there are places where changes could be made to reduce the heat island effect. Write a letter to city officials to tell them about your ideas.

North of the Border:

Are Nonnative Species Moving Northward As the Climate Changes?

What Kinds of Scientists Did This Research?

botanist: This scientist studies plants.

ecologist: This scientist studies organisms and their relationship with their living and nonliving environment.

Thinking About Science

As science advances over time, new scientific questions are continually discovered. Many of the scientific questions asked today would have been unthinkable even ten years ago. Every time a team of scientists learns something new, the new finding creates new questions. New technology, in addition, enables scientists to explore questions that could not have been explored in the past. The world of science, therefore, keeps expanding. Now is an exciting time to be a scientist. The future will bring even more opportunities for scientific exploration.

Thinking About the Environment

Plants and nonhuman animals live in a particular range, or area. Range is determined by many factors. Some of these factors include temperature, amount of rainfall, soil type, and **elevation**. The scientists in this research identified plant and animal species' ranges by latitude (FIG. 1).

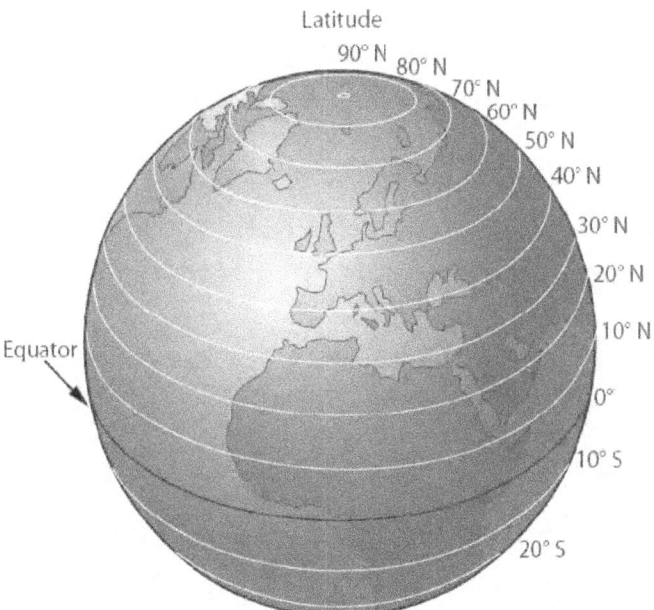

FIGURE 1. LATITUDE MEASUREMENTS ARE TAKEN BY OBSERVING IMAGINARY LINES ON EARTH'S SURFACE FROM THE EQUATOR TO THE POLES. EACH IMAGINARY LINE OF LATITUDE IS NUMBERED. THESE MEASUREMENTS ENABLE SCIENTISTS TO EXACTLY IDENTIFY AREAS ON EARTH BETWEEN THE EQUATOR AND THE POLES. AREAS CLOSE TO THE EQUATOR ARE WARMER THAN AREAS CLOSE TO THE POLES.
ILLUSTRATION BY SAMANTHA BOND.

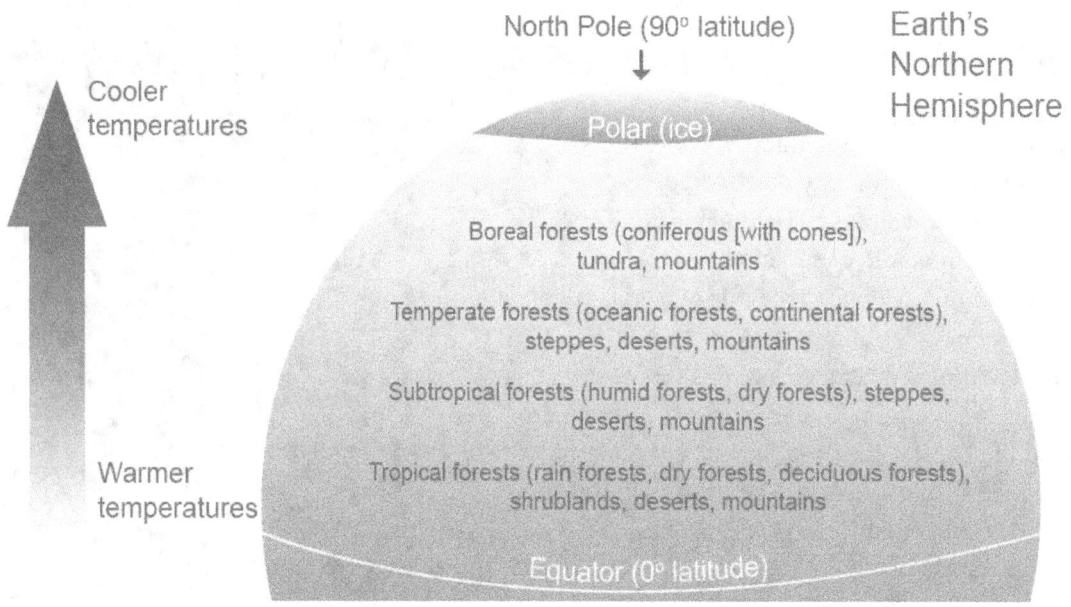

FIGURE 2. TROPICAL PLANTS GROW IN AREAS CLOSE TO THE EQUATOR. LAND LYING FARTHER FROM THE EQUATOR HAS DIFFERENT TYPES OF PLANTS. AREAS WITH DIFFERENT TYPES OF PLANTS ARE BROADLY CLASSIFIED AS TROPICAL, SUBTROPICAL, TEMPERATE, AND BOREAL.

Scientists can determine the highest and lowest latitude in which a species lives in a particular area. Areas close to the equator are warm, and areas close to the poles are cold. The average weather, or climate, affects the type of vegetation growing in an area (FIG. 2). Although many factors affect the range of plants and animals, latitude is one way to define a species' range.

Introduction

Nonnative plant and animal species live in areas where they are not naturally found. These species were brought to new areas on purpose or by mistake. Nonnative plants, for example, may have been brought to a new area on purpose to help beautify an area. Harmful insects, on the other hand, might have moved to a new area by riding on a wooden packing crate. These insects were brought to the new area by mistake. Some nonnative species live and survive in a new area without human help. Scientists call these nonnative species naturalized (**na** chə rə **līzd**).

Number Crunch

A circle has 360 degrees. How many degrees of latitude are found between the North Pole and the South Pole? (Hint: The area between the North Pole and the South Pole is one half of a circle.)

A nonnative species becomes naturalized by successfully competing with native species. Naturalized species compete with native species for food, water, sunlight, space, and other resources. This competition can harm native species and can change the native ecosystem. Scientists want to understand and predict the impact of nonnative species. To do this, scientists need to know where these species become naturalized.

A naturalized species has two ranges. The first range is the one where the species lives in its native habitat. The second range is the one where the species is naturalized, surviving in a nonnative area without the help of humans. A species' range is limited by its ability to survive in different climates. Species, therefore, are more able to survive east to west across the globe, but are limited by latitude. The scientists in this study wanted to answer this question: Are naturalized species' latitudinal ranges the same, larger, or smaller than their native ranges?

Reflection Section

Reflection Section

 Describe the problem caused by naturalized species.

 Should humans care about what happens to native species? Why or why not?

Methods

The scientists used **databases** that identify the ranges of 744 plant, bird, and **mammal** species. Bird and mammal species were introduced globally across different continents. Some plant species were brought from eastern Asia to the United States (FIG. 3). The naturalized United States species included 147 bird species, 85 mammal species, and 512 plant species (FIGS. 4-9).

Meet the Scientist

Hong Qian,
BOTANIST AND ECOLOGIST:

My favorite science experience is finding out what causes different species to live in different areas worldwide. One of the most interesting questions is what causes the "latitudinal diversity gradient." Over 200 years ago, scientists noticed that many different species live in and near tropical regions. In habitats closer to the poles, however, fewer different species are found. Causes of the latitudinal diversity gradient are not well known. In my research, I explore how **evolutionary** processes and **ecological** factors interact to influence global patterns of species diversity.

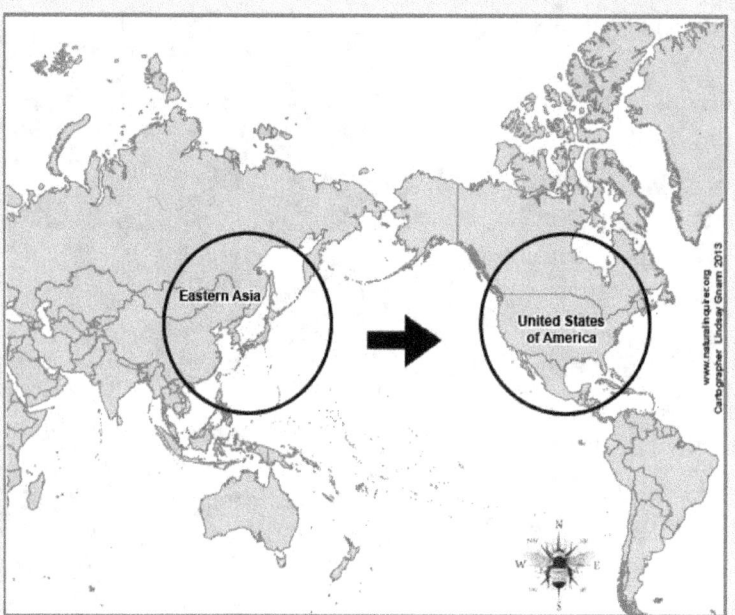

FIGURE 3. THE SCIENTISTS STUDIED THE NATIVE AND NATURALIZED LATITUDINAL RANGES OF PLANTS BROUGHT FROM EASTERN ASIA TO THE UNITED STATES. MAP BY LINDSAY GNANN.

FIGURE 4. CATTLE EGRET. PHOTO COURTESY OF JOY VIOLA, NORTHEASTERN UNIVERSITY, AND HTTP://WWW.BUGWOOD.ORG

FIGURE 5. EUROPEAN STARLING. PHOTO COURTESY OF LEE KARNEY, U.S. FISH AND WILDLIFE SERVICE, AND HTTP://WWW.BUGWOOD.ORG.

FIGURE 6. BLACK-TAILED JACKRABBIT. PHOTO COURTESY OF THE U.S. FISH AND WILDLIFE SERVICE ARCHIVE, AND HTTP://WWW.BUGWOOD.ORG.

FIGURE 7. COMMON BRUSH-TAIL POSSUM. PHOTO COURTESY OF ALFRED VIOLA, NORTHEASTERN UNIVERSITY, AND HTTP://WWW.BUGWOOD.ORG.

FIGURE 8. GARLIC MUSTARD. PHOTO COURTESY OF CHRIS EVANS, ILLINOIS WILDLIFE ACTION PLAN, AND HTTP://WWW.BUGWOOD.ORG.

FIGURE 9. KUDZU. PHOTO COURTESY OF JAMES H. MILLER AND TED BODNER, SOUTHERN WEED SCIENCE SOCIETY, AND HTTP://WWW.BUGWOOD.ORG.

For each plant and animal species, the scientists recorded:

- The northernmost latitude of the species' native range.

- The southernmost latitude of the species' native range.

- The northernmost latitude of the species' naturalized range.

- The southernmost latitude of the species' naturalized range.

Because latitude is expressed in numbers, the scientists were able to calculate certain things. From the northernmost and southernmost latitudes, the scientists calculated the midpoint of the range. The scientists also calculated the extent of each species' range. The extent is the total distance between the northernmost and southernmost latitudes.

The scientists wanted to know three things:

1. Are naturalized species found in latitudes higher, lower, or the same as their native latitudes?

2. What percentage of species' naturalized ranges shifted toward the poles, toward the equator, or in both directions as compared with their native ranges (FIG. 10)?

3. Does a significant difference exist in the extent of naturalized ranges as compared with native ranges?

FIGURE 10. FOUR WAYS A NATURALIZED RANGE COULD SHIFT AS COMPARED WITH A NATIVE RANGE. ILLUSTRATION BY STEPHANIE PFEIFFER.

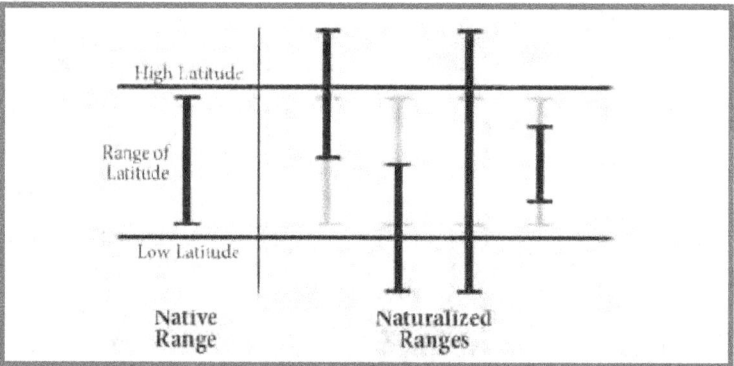

Reflection Section

⇨ How did the scientists calculate the midpoint of the ranges?

⇨ Look at figure 10. This figure shows four ways the range of naturalized species could shift as compared with their native range. Do you think it is possible that the naturalized range might not shift at all? Why?

Findings

The scientists found that the range midpoint for all species was similar for native and naturalized ranges. Of the species studied, individual plants showed the greatest similarity between their midpoints, followed by mammals and then birds. While the **average** midpoint might have been similar, individual bird species showed more variety in their midpoints overall.

In every case, however, the midpoint of the naturalized range was a bit higher than the native range midpoint (FIG. 11).

Species	Degrees Latitude
Birds	0.23 degrees higher
Mammals	3.83 degrees higher
Plants introduced from Asia to North America	2.47 degrees higher

FIGURE 11. THE AVERAGE MIDPOINT OF THE NATURALIZED RANGE, COMPARED WITH THE NATIVE RANGE, IN DEGREES OF LATITUDE.

Legend for Figure 12

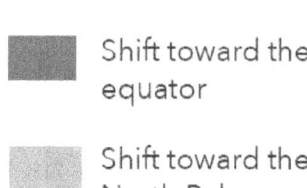
■ Shift toward the equator

■ Shift toward the North Pole

Shift toward the North Pole and the equator

■ No shift

Most species either shifted their naturalized range toward the North Pole or did not shift their range (FIG. 12).

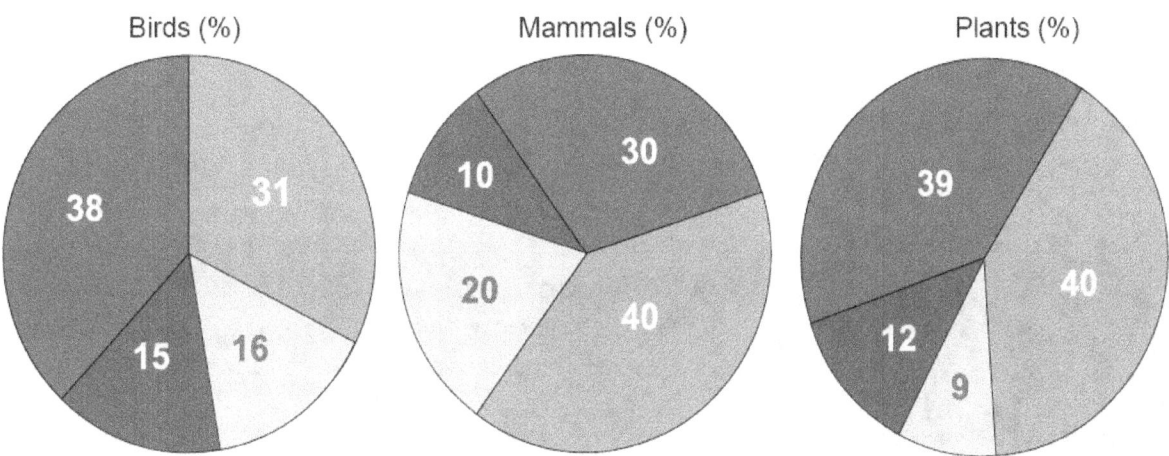

Birds (%) — 38, 31, 15, 16

Mammals (%) — 30, 10, 20, 40

Plants (%) — 39, 40, 12, 9

FIGURE 12. PERCENTAGE OF SHIFTING IN NATURALIZED RANGES COMPARED WITH NATIVE RANGES.

FIGURE **13.** THE RANGE EXTENT WAS GREATER FOR SPECIES IN THEIR NATIVE RANGES.

The native range extent for most species was greater than their naturalized range extent. In other words, most native species lived across more degrees of latitude than the same species living in a naturalized range (FIG. 13).

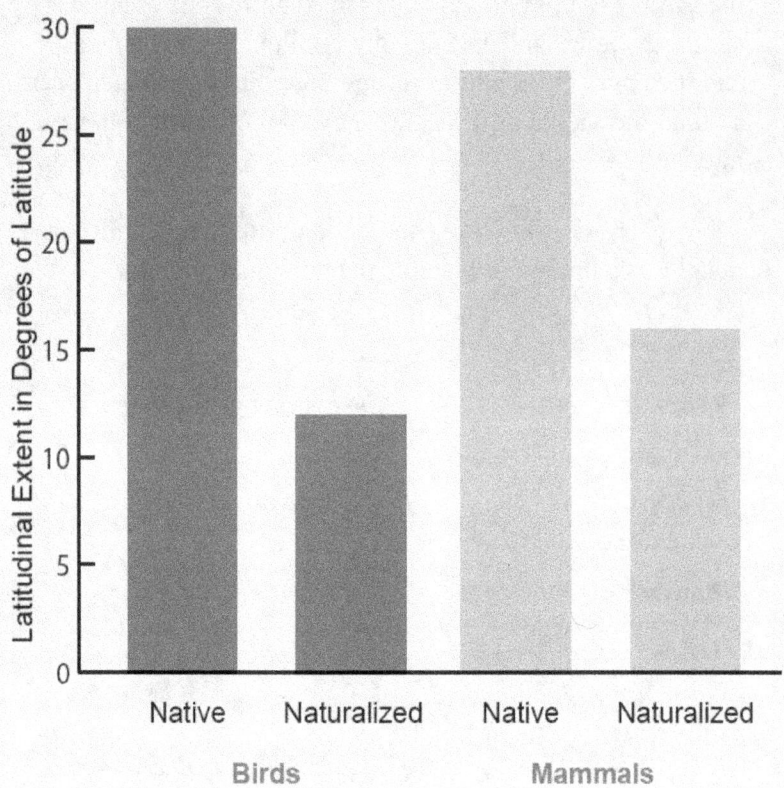

Reflection Section
Reflection Section

 For the most part, the range of naturalized species either did not shift or shifted toward the North Pole as compared with native ranges. Why might some of the ranges shift toward the North Pole?

 The midpoint of naturalized ranges was similar to the midpoint of native ranges for all species. What is one possible explanation?

Discussion

The scientists were particularly **intrigued** by one of their findings. They noted that bird, mammal, and plant species showed a slight shift in the North Pole's direction in their naturalized range. The scientists do not know why this is happening, but they have some ideas.

Humans might have introduced more nonnative species to higher latitudes across the United States than in lower latitudes. This introduction of more nonnative species would mean more naturalized species live in higher latitudes.

Another possible explanation involves climate change. Climate change has meant warmer temperatures across the United States.

Mammals and birds, which can easily move from place to place, may be moving north as the climate warms. Naturalized species, furthermore, may be more responsive to climate change than native species. This responsiveness may be true because naturalized species are not **constrained** by **predators** and competitors. In their native habitat, species evolve together to create a balance between predators and **prey.**

The nature of scientific study may also play a role. Newer studies of naturalized species include climate change effects. Older studies of native species' ranges may not include climate change. It may be that newer studies of native species' ranges would reflect a northern shift as well.

The findings show that when a species' native range is large, its naturalized range is also large. If no other information is available, this finding can help scientists predict the future range of naturalizing nonnative species. In addition, the findings show that naturalized ranges are, in general, smaller than native ranges. This finding could mean that naturalized species will continue to expand their range over time.

The scientists believe that species' range shift in the North Pole's direction is important. This shift may mean that the mix of species in higher latitudes will change in the future. More naturalized species at higher latitudes will cause northern ecosystems to change. These changes will place more stress on native species, which are already under stress from climate change.

Adapted from Guo, Q.; Sax, D.; Qian, H.; Early, R. 2012. Latitudinal shifts of introduced species: possible causes and implications. Biological Invasions. 14: 547–556. http://www.srs fs.usda.gov/pubs/ja/2012/ja_2012_guo_002.pdf.

Reflection Section

 How do the scientists think climate change may be affecting species' naturalized ranges?

 What might happen to northern native species and ecosystems as naturalized species move northward?

Glossary

average (**a** v(ə-)rij): The number determined by dividing the sum of two or more quantities by the number of quantities added.

constrain (kən **strān**): To hold in or keep back by force.

database (**dā** tə **bās**): A comprehensive collection of related data organized for convenient access, generally in a computer.

ecological (**e** kä **lä** ji kəl): Having to do with ecology. Ecology is the study of the relationship of living things with each other and their environment.

elevation (**e** lə **vā** shən): The height above sea level.

evolutionary (**e** və **lü** shən er ē): Of, relating to, or produced by evolution. Evolution is the process of continuous change from a lower, simpler, or worse state to a higher, more complex, or better state.

habitat (**ha** bə tat): The place or environment where a plant or animal naturally or normally lives and grows.

intrigue (in **trēg**): To arouse the interest, desire, or curiosity of.

mammal (**ma** məl): Any warm-blooded animal with a backbone and glands to produce milk for feeding their young.

native (**nā** tiv): Living or growing naturally in a particular region.

predator (**pre** də tər): An animal that preys on other animals for food.

prey (**prā**): An animal, including insects, taken by a predator for food.

tropics (**trä** piks): The region that surrounds the equator and goes from 23.5 degrees north latitude to 23.5 degrees south latitude.

vertical (**vər** ti kəl): Going straight up or down from a surface.

Accented syllables are in **bold**. Marks and definitions are from http://www.merriam-webster.com.

JACK-IN-THE-PULPIT IS A NATIVE SPECIES. PHOTO BY BABS McDONALD.

FACTivity

Time Needed
30-40 minutes

Materials
- The data table provided in this FACTivity
- The two blank graphs provided in this FACTivity
- Pencil and thin black felt marker
- Piece of blank paper or science notebook
- Ruler (optional)

The question you will answer in this FACTivity is: What are general patterns, if any, between the native and naturalized ranges of 25 plant species?

Methods

You will plot the native range and naturalized range of 25 plants on a graph. Note that these data are actual data provided to you by the scientists in this study. For each plant, place a dot on the graph at the southern and northern limits of its range. The degrees in latitude are given on the Y axis. (The y axis is on the left). Draw a dark vertical line with the felt marker to connect the two dots for each plant. See the example graph on page 85 before beginning.

After you have finished completing both graphs, compare the two. Identify and write three observations about the overall patterns you see, using complete sentences, correct punctuation, and proper grammar.

THE MIMOSA TREE IS A NONNATIVE SPECIES. PHOTO BY JAMES H. MILLER, U.S. FOREST SERVICE, AND COURTESY OF HTTP://WWW.BUGWOOD.ORG.

Plant Number	Native Range in Degrees Latitude		Naturalized Range in Degrees Latitude	
	Southern Limit	Northern Limit	Southern Limit	Northern Limit
1	23.0	52.0	28.0	54.5
2	27.5	47.0	37.5	40.3
3	23.0	50.0	43.0	45.2
4	44.0	48.2	34.1	65.0
5	55.0	55.0	31.2	54.2
6	23.0	47.0	28.0	54.2
7	23.0	25.5	28.0	28.0
8	25.2	63.0	63.3	63.3
9	23.0	47.0	31.3	54.5
10	42.0	42.0	40.0	63.3
11	37.5	47.5	41.5	44.7
12	36.0	63.0	43.0	43.0
13	42.0	63.0	33.5	54.0
14	38.1	55.5	28.0	63.3
15	30.0	47.0	37.5	49.0
16	23.0	25.2	28.0	28.0
17	42.0	47.0	34.1	54.5
18	37.7	48.2	31.2	54.5
19	23.0	38.1	28.0	38.8
20	23.0	26.9	31.2	47.2
21	32.0	63.0	37.5	43.0
22	23.0	66.5	28.0	65.0
23	23.0	29.1	28.0	33.5
24	35.5	63.0	37.5	65.0
25	42.0	58.0	31.2	65.0

Example Graph

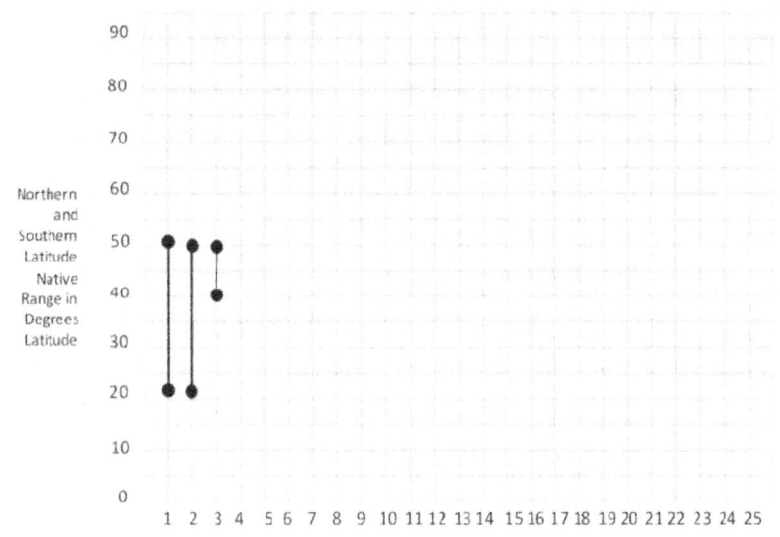

Your teacher will lead a class discussion with the following question:

How do your observations compare with the scientists' observations for native and naturalized plant ranges and why?

NATIVE RANGE

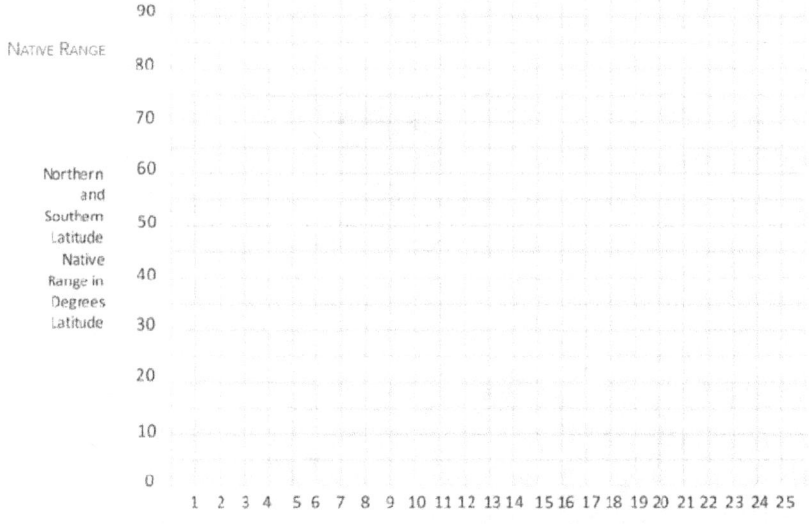

NATURALIZED RANGE

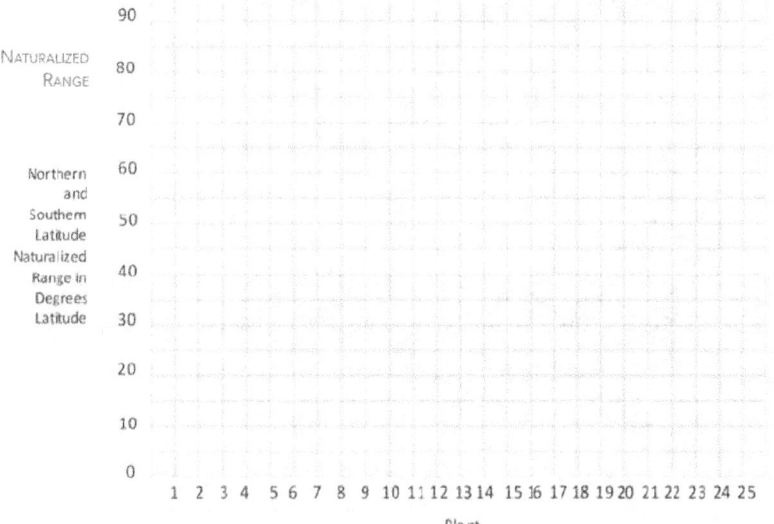

Plant

If you are a Project Learning Tree-trained educator, you may use *Invasive Species,* as an additional resource.

FACTivity Extension

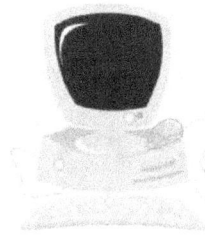

Calculate the range extent (in both ranges) for each of the 25 plants by adding the southern latitudinal limit to the northern latitudinal limit. Calculate the average latitudinal extent. Calculate the average for both the native and naturalized ranges. What pattern do you see between the two averages?

Web Resources

Eastern Forest Threat Assessment Center Bookmarks
http://www.forestthreats.org/products/bookmarks

Eastern Forest Threat Assessment Center Fact Sheets
http://www.forestthreats.org/products/fact-sheets

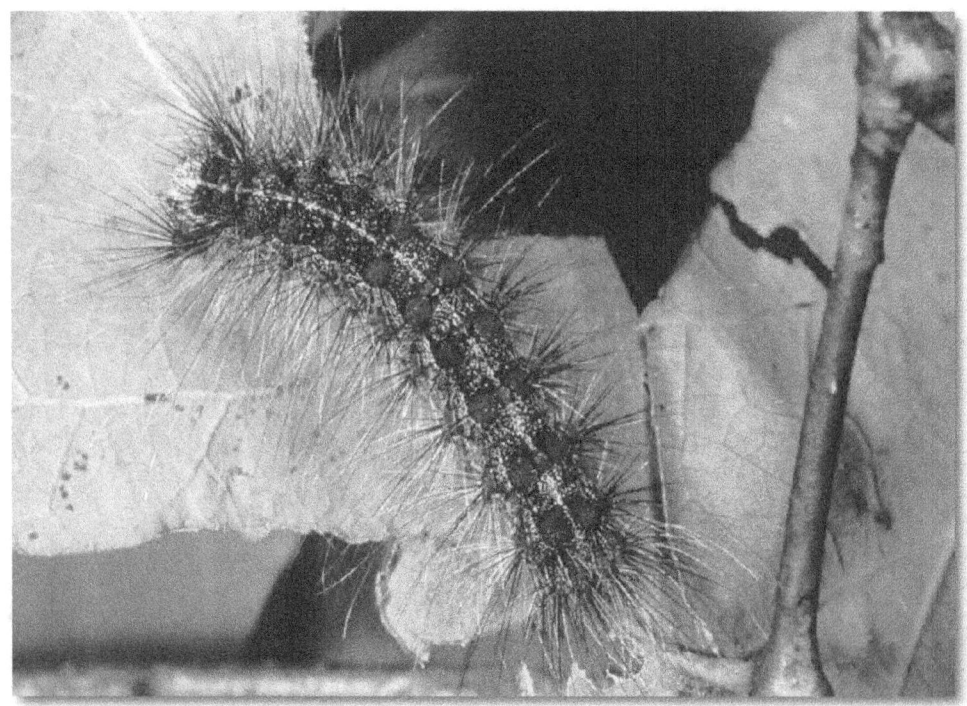

THE GYPSY MOTH CATERPILLAR IS A NONNATIVE SPECIES. PHOTO BY U.S. FISH AND WILDLIFE SERVICE JAMES APPLEBY, UNIVERSITY OF ILLINOIS.

Southern United States Climate Change
Photo Challenge

Common Core Connection

EACH OF THE FOLLOWING PHOTOS APPEARED IN ONE
OF THE ARTICLES IN THIS JOURNAL. EXPLAIN WHAT EACH OF THESE
PHOTOS MEANS. YOU MAY WRITE YOUR EXPLANATION OR HOLD A
CLASS DISCUSSION. IF YOU WRITE YOUR EXPLANATION, USE COMPLETE
SENTENCES WITH PROPER GRAMMAR, SPELLING, AND PUNCTUATION.

PHOTO COURTESY OF GILA NATIONAL FOREST.

PHOTO COURTESY OF JOY VIOLA, NORTHEASTERN UNIVERSITY,
AND HTTP://WWW.BUGWOOD.ORG.

PHOTO COURTESY OF HANQIN TIAN.

PHOTO BY BABS MCDONALD.

PHOTOS BY BABS MCDONALD.

Southern United States Climate Change Crossword Puzzle

Across

2. The science or practice of preparing the soil, producing crops, and raising livestock.
4. To make an assumption to test its logical consequences.
5. Action taken to cause something to be less harsh, hostile, or severe.
6. To break up and scatter or vanish.
7. To bring to an end.
10. To hold in or keep back by force.
12. The place or environment where a plant or animal lives and grows.
13. The height above sea level.
14. Something that is able or apt to vary.
15. A period of dry weather with little or no rain.

Down

1. Rain, hail, snow, mist, or sleet.
3. The average in a set of numbers.
8. To stop or interrupt the progress or intended course of something.
9. Outside of the city.
11. A substance that plants, animals, and people need to live and grow.

National Education Standards

Which National Science Education Standards Can Be Addressed by These Articles?

	Everything But the Carbon Sink	Flow Down!	Fire and Water	Wide Open Spaces	North of the Border
Science as Inquiry					
Abilities Necessary To Do Scientific Inquiry	✓	✓	✓	✓	✓
Understandings About Scientific Inquiry	✓	✓	✓	✓	✓
Life Science					
Structure and Function in Living Systems	✓	✓		✓	
Regulation & Behavior		✓		✓	✓
Populations & Ecosystems	✓		✓		✓
Diversity & Adaptations of Organisms		✓		✓	✓
Earth Science					
Structure of Earth System	✓				✓
Science & Technology					
Understandings About Science & Technology		✓		✓	
Science in Personal & Social Perspectives					
Risks & Benefits			✓		
Science & Technology in Society	✓	✓	✓	✓	
Natural Hazards		✓	✓	✓	
History & Nature of Science					
Science as a Human Endeavor	✓	✓	✓	✓	✓
Nature of Science	✓	✓	✓	✓	✓

Which National Curriculum Standards for Social Studies Can Be Addressed by These Articles?

	Everything But the Carbon Sink	Flow Down!	Fire and Water	Wide Open Spaces	North of the Border
Culture				🐝	🐝
Time, Continuity, and Change	🐝	🐝	🐝	🐝	🐝
People, Places, and Environments	🐝	🐝	🐝	🐝	🐝
Individuals, Groups, and Institutions				🐝	
Production, Distribution, and Consumption	🐝				
Science, Technology, and Society	🐝	🐝	🐝	🐝	
Global Connections	🐝	🐝	🐝		🐝

PHOTO BY BAES MCDONALD.

What Is the Forest Service?

The Forest Service is a part of the United States Department of Agriculture (USDA). It is made up of thousands of people who care for the Nation's forest land. The Forest Service manages over 150 national forests and almost 20 national grasslands. These are large areas of trees, streams, and grasslands. National forests are similar in some ways to national parks. Both are public lands, meaning that they are owned by the public and managed for the public's use and benefit. Both national forests and national parks provide clean water, homes for the animals that live in the wild, and places for people to do fun things in the outdoors. National forests also provide resources for people to use, such as trees for lumber, minerals, and plants used for medicines. Some people in the Forest Service are scientists whose work is presented in the journal. Forest Service scientists work to solve problems and provide new information about natural resources so that we can make sure our natural environment is healthy, now and into the future.

Learn more about the Forest Service by visiting http://www.fs.fed.us.

What Is the Southern Research Station?

The Southern Research Station is part of Forest Service Research and Development. Headquartered in Asheville, North Carolina, the station serves 13 Southern States and beyond. The Southern Research Station's mission is to create the science and technology needed to sustain and enhance southern forest ecosystems and the benefits they provide. Since the beginning of the 20th Century, the Southern Research Station's 130 researchers have excelled in studies on temperate and tropical forests, forest resources, and forest products. These studies provide a wealth of long-term information on the dynamics of tree plantations and natural stands, watersheds, and wildlife habitats.

Learn more about the Southern Research Station by visiting http://www.srs.fs.usda.gov.

What Is the Cradle of Forestry in America Interpretive Association?

The Cradle of Forestry in America Interpretive Association is a 501(c)3 nonprofit organization based out of Brevard, NC. The Interpretive Association strives to help people better understand ecology through recreation and education opportunities. Their projects include:

- Campground and recreation area management
- Educational programs and services, including *Natural Inquirer*, *Investi-gator*, *Natural IQ*, and *Nature-Oriented Parenting*
- Sales of forest-related gifts and educational materials
- Workshops, newsletters, and publications
- Partnership with the Forest Service to provide programming at the Cradle of Forestry Historic Site

Learn more about the Cradle of Forestry in America Interpretive Association by visiting http://www.cfaia.org.

Ms. Lewis's 7th grade class, Rosman Middle School, Brevard North Carolina

Visit these Web sites for more information:

Natural Inquirer
http://www.naturalinquirer.org

Investi-gator
http://www.scienceinvestigator.org

Forest Service Conservation Education
http://www.fs.usda.gov/conservationeducation

Discover the Forest
http://discovertheforest.org/

Cradle of Forestry in America Interpretive Association
http://www.cfaia.org

Environmental Protection Agency Climate Change Future
http://www.epa.gov/climatechange/science/future.html

Project Learning Tree
http://www.plt.org

Follow us on Facebook https://www.facebook.com/NaturalInquirer and Twitter!